M000303106

NEVER ENOUGHITIS

NEVER
ENOUGHITIS

A STORY OF SUCCESS, EMPTINESS, AND OVERCOMING MYSELF

ROBERT ALTHUIS

ROBERT ALTHUIS

LIONCREST

PUBLISHING

COPYRIGHT © 2020 SACRED GRACE TRUST

All rights reserved.

NEVER ENOUGHITIS

A Story of Success, Emptiness, and Overcoming Myself

ISBN   978-1-5445-1806-0 *Hardcover*

      978-1-5445-1805-3 *Paperback*

      978-1-5445-1804-6 *Ebook*

To my mom, for being the biggest believer in me.

To my father, for unknowingly being my greatest teacher.

To my three beautiful children and Cara, their badass mom. It took me some hard knocks and deep lows to fully realize and embrace they are the true gift of my life.

And to Beautiful, for making me believe in love again.

CONTENTS

INTRODUCTION

I n hindsight, I had plenty of wake-up calls, plenty of signs that my moral compass had lost its magnetic north. I just hadn't listened.

One red flag came when I was having dinner with two brothers I had met in Colombia. Both men were connected with the US embassy. I suspected the older brother, Gustavo, worked with the secret service, though I never conclusively confirmed that suspicion.

We were eating at Salto del Angel, a prominent restaurant in a busy section of town about a block from my apartment. During the course of our meal, I asked Gustavo about a recent high-profile "liquidation" that had occurred in front of Salto del Angel. He described in almost too much detail how liquidations like this are executed with flawless choreography.

"When they're done in a busy area like this, it's to make a statement," Gustavo said. "Some businessmen get trapped in the nets of the mafia, and they don't realize it until it's too late."

Gustavo spoke more freely than he ever had, and I hung on his every word. The stories all had a grim undertone. The cold-hearted violence he described was straight out of a suspense thriller. It seemed unreal.

"There are still dangerous places in Colombia," Gustavo said. "There are people you don't want to get involved with. You don't want to go on their turf."

Gustavo's tone had changed, and I sensed he was trying to tell me something. I had recently started evaluating a project in the port of Buenaventura, the largest Colombian port on the Pacific Ocean, and a notorious hotbed of the cocaine export trade. Lord knows how Gustavo even knew about my new project; then again, he was in the business of knowing things.

Gustavo continued. "Sometimes businessmen get swept up into their web. If these people need something from you or want you to go away, they have their own ways of taking care of it, and they're not going to hire a lawyer. These people don't play by the same rules you and I do."

That night, Gustavo's words fell on deaf ears. I was blinded by my relentless pursuit of *more* and *bigger*. Within a few weeks, however, the message that I was encroaching on dangerous turf became loud and clear. A group of bad actors started to show their muscle and unleashed a host of scare tactics on me that, to this day, I don't discuss with people. But the intimidations were bone-chilling. I started looking over my shoulder everywhere I went: as I walked to my armored car, as I pulled into the garage, as I took the elevator to my apartment.

After weeks of living in this traumatized state, I couldn't take it anymore. I finagled my way out of the project and, shortly thereafter, sold my various business interests in Colombia. Despite making millions on this sale and despite already being a multi-millionaire from years of business accomplishments, I returned to Miami feeling empty and disillusioned. On the outside, I was a great success—I had achieved all the worldly things I thought would make me happy—but inside, I was a broken man. At home, I was brought face-to-face with my crumbling marriage, which only sank me deeper into my black hole of sorrow and despair. I was a lost soul.

Landing at rock bottom doesn't happen overnight—especially when rock bottom is this deep. It's the final station on a slow path of wrong turns and poor decisions guided by an egoic mind gone awry.

A VERY LUCKY GUY

My story starts 5,500 miles from Colombia in a beautiful country called the Netherlands. I was born on the right side of the tracks and grew up about thirty minutes outside Amsterdam in a quaint, idyllic village surrounded by gorgeous forests and wide-open farmland. In the 1970s and 80s, the Netherlands was a prosperous, safe place, and I enjoyed incredible freedoms in my childhood. From the age of five or six, I rode my bike everywhere: to school, to friends' houses, to play sports—you name it. My father was a successful executive, my mother owned her own store, and I was the youngest of three boys, so I was given a lot of leeway.

At age eighteen, I left home to attend college in Amsterdam and took full advantage of my newfound freedom. I partied like a rock star, cut class (I think I made it to four classes that first year), and did a lot of things that will ensure I never get elected to public office.

Toward the end of my first year, I fell madly in love with a girl who was a much more dedicated student. Perhaps I cleaned up my act to wow her—or maybe it happened by osmosis—but the end result was that I got more serious about school and managed to obtain an associate's degree in economics and political science.

At the end of my third year of college, my thirst for adventure kicked in, and I was off to Australia, leaving behind a fizzled romance and an unfinished bachelor's degree. For the next year, I backpacked from Sydney to Perth, skippered a yacht around the Whitsunday Islands, drove a passenger bus in Hervey Bay, and had stints as a construction worker, banana picker, and bartender. It was epic.

After Australia, I flew to Los Angeles, bought a motorcycle, and drove across the country. Over the next few years, I tried to break into the professional tennis circuit, but alas, I was a day late and a dollar short. Pursuing this boyhood dream brought me a lot of great stories, but I was never able to truly break through.

At age twenty-five, I finally landed in Atlanta, where I got a job in real estate starting at seven bucks an hour. I thrived in that arena, and within three years, I was making six figures. I also attended night school at Georgia State University, graduating summa cum laude with a BBA in real estate. From there, I was accepted to Columbia Business School in New York City, and fueled (or blinded) by ambition and excitement, I charged ahead and started my MBA program in January 2001.

While starting my new life in Atlanta, I fell in love with a smart and captivating trial lawyer. Not long after, we married and embarked on a rollercoaster relationship. She was equally ambitious and had no desire to sit for the New York bar or sideline her career while I pursued my MBA, and by the time I graduated, it was clear to both of us that our paths had already separated. By June of 2002, I was newly single and about to kick off my postgraduate career at GE, one of America's most venerable blue chip companies.

Which brings us to the true beginning of this tale of pure love, driving ambition, glorious success, ruthless failure, and dark depression—and the journey within that brought me the happiness and peace I had been seeking all along.

MEMOIR-HELP

I started writing this book as self-therapy, as medicine to get me through some of the most painful moments and deepest lows of my life. I wrote it to heal myself from overwhelming heartbreak, anxiety, and despair so intense at times, I couldn't breathe.

As I wrote, however, I realized this book could serve a greater purpose. I'm not the only person to follow ambition, seek success, pursue money, and chase happiness in external things only to find that those things—more and more money, fancy cars, big houses, luxury vacations, even having the perfect family—never give you lasting fulfillment once you have them. I'm not the only person to feel empty, stuck, lost, crushed by disillusionment, and constantly wondering, "Is this all there is?" And I'm not the only person to numb the hollow, empty feeling with myriad distractions.

The truth is, to varying degrees, we all suffer from what I call *never enoughitis*: we seek, succeed, accomplish, earn, pursue, and accumulate, but it's never enough to satisfy our deepest longings and give us true happiness. So we get a better job to make more money and buy more toys and a bigger house and go on more exotic vacations—but it's never enough. We try numbing the pain with exercise, hobbies, partying, sex, porn, alcohol, painkillers, and maybe even an affair.

But it's never fucking enough.

As I learned, never enoughitis cannot be healed through external things; the answer lies within. Finding the fulfillment, peace, and happiness we all seek requires a fundamental shift in our awareness and consciousness. We need to transform the way we see ourselves and the world, as well as the way in which we live and move in that world. Curing never enoughitis is ultimately about making a fundamental shift from living a life of greed to living a life of grace. It's the shift from self-interest to service to others, from fear and lack to love and abundance, from being played by the game to being a game changer, from chasing nothingness to creating impact fueled by a deep sense of purpose. The good news is this powerful transformation is readily available to everyone.

I am not the same person I was five years ago. Through my spiritual journey—a relentless soul-search for the truth coupled with intensive therapy, healing old wounds, deep introspection, and new daily choices—I have been able to leave my past in the past, which has opened up the path to forgiveness and radical change.

Through my story and the lessons learned, I want to help you experience the same fundamental shift. I want to help you see that you're not a fixed asset, hardwired in a certain way, and the world isn't either. By taking a journey within, you can reinvent yourself, reprogram your life, and experience the wholeness you seek. And by changing yourself, you will not simply change your world; you will change the world at large.

I like to think of this book as memoir-help. Parts 1 and 2 are memoir, chronicling my life's highest peaks and lowest valleys. In part 1, "Fairy-Tale Stuff," I talk about the woman who took my breath away, our beautiful courtship, our blissful marriage, and my simultaneous steady career advancement. In part 2, "Real Life," I share how it all slowly, painfully fell apart, regardless (or because!) of the worldly success I had achieved. In the end, I came face-to-face with my never enoughitis as a shattered, disillusioned, empty man. I spent five months in therapy and took a journey within that taught me the life-changing lessons covered in part 3, "Phoenix Rising." Each chapter in this self-help section discusses a transformative lesson, explores how it manifested in my own life, and ends with questions to help you navigate your own journey within.

I wrote this book for men like me: the quintessential alpha male, the seeker of adventure with an insatiable drive to compete and measure up against anyone and anything, the modern-day warrior who denies his deepest fears, who never learned to share or fully express his true feelings, and who views vulnerability as a weakness he cannot afford in this dog-eat-dog world.

Men, you have been raised to believe that fully expressing yourself makes you weak. I want to give you permission to stop quashing your deepest feelings and emotions, to open up and let yourself feel. I hope you find the truth I did: that your greatest strength and true power reside in living from the heart, not the mind.

To my female readers, perhaps my story will help you understand the alpha male in your life. More importantly, I hope you find answers for your own never enoughitis, and that you learn to embrace your powerful, exquisite feminine energy.

No matter who you are, if you feel stuck, empty, unfulfilled, or at the end of your rope, if you are not finding the true satisfaction and fulfillment you seek or are lacking the clarity of purpose and meaning you crave, I hope you find answers in my story. You may find that the answers are new and esoteric and out there. But if what you're currently doing isn't working, what have you got to lose?

PART I

FAIRY-TALE STUFF

The madness of love is the greatest of heaven's blessings.

—PLATO

I MEET HER

I still remember the dress she wore when I first saw her.

It was June 2002. I had just started an executive management program at GE after graduating from Columbia Business School a month earlier. For the first of my four, six-month rotations, I had been assigned to GE Energy Financial Services in Stamford, Connecticut. After two weeks in Stamford, I headed to Crotonville, New York, for my first two-week executive management training.

Located a little north of New York City, Crotonville is a very special place and part of GE's rich history and corporate folklore. Imagine a world-class hotel and conference center, kitchenettes stocked with snacks and drinks, an onsite bar called the White House, fantastic training facilities and running trails, and of course, a helipad, all in a gorgeous setting with manicured landscaping. This is where GE's prodigies and senior management come to learn, train, and soak up the corporate culture. It's truly a magnificent place.

We had all reported the night before. Some people had already found and checked out the White House, but most of us were

Crotonville rookies and had gone to bed early to get ready for the big opening day. Now I was sitting in a giant auditorium about ten minutes before the eight o'clock start time. There was a buzz of excitement in the room packed with revved-up go-getters recruited from inside GE as well as all the top echelon schools in the nation.

As I sat there with my morning cup of coffee, I felt a little jaded. Yes, the facilities were impressive, and all the people I had met so far were terrific. But having just spent the last eighteen months in stage auditoriums identical to this one, I wasn't too excited about more lecture-type learning. I was ready to *do*.

So, a little bored, I sat there watching as the auditorium slowly filled up. The stage in this auditorium was down in the pit, as they called it, and the rows and rows of long tables configured in a U shape around the pit were staggered in elevation. I sat alongside the stairs, high up on the left side of the middle section, maybe three rows down from the top and a good six or seven rows up from the pit.

Then, for no particular reason, I looked back up the stairs, and my eyes locked on this beautiful girl with a gorgeous smile. Don't ask me why I looked up—I think these things are preordained, to tell you the truth—but I was instantly mesmerized. I couldn't take my eyes off her pretty face, disarming smile, dark-brown eyes, and olive skin. She was wearing an incredibly elegant light-brown dress with white polka dots that accentuated her petite, perfectly proportioned figure.

I watched her take every single step down; it was like a scene unfolding in slow motion. My eyes followed her to her seat a row or two down from me and to the left side of the stairs that separated the long tables. I'm sure there were incredible speakers, but I don't recall anything from that first day at Crotonville, except the path she took from the top of the stairs to her seat. Right there and then, I became as alert and razor-focused as a gladiator going into the arena: I was going to get to know this person.

Over the next two weeks, the attendees were often split up into groups, and as luck would have it, she and I were never put in the same group. I saw her regularly, and each glimpse hit me like a bolt of lightning. I was swept off my feet, and I didn't even know her name.

Every day, I looked for opportunities to talk to her. I saw her at the gym, but she was usually on the treadmill or otherwise unapproachable. I went to the White House every night, but when I did see her, she was engaged in conversation, or I was stuck in a mad game of Ping Pong. I finally managed to introduce myself and learn her name was Cara, but to my chagrin, she had no eyes for me. I had played the field enough to know that despite two weeks of trying, I didn't even make it on her radar.

Not to worry, though; there were more trainings to come. Rome wasn't built in a day.

SHE MEETS ME

I n late August 2002, we had a second training, this time a week-long course in Atlanta, Georgia. I arrived a few days early to take care of some housekeeping business and catch up with old friends. A few late-night benders later, I reported for training at the Marriott Marquis Hotel in downtown Atlanta.

This training was very different from the two-week-long event in Crotonville. First, a 1,000-person nondescript conference hotel does not exactly offer the same ambience as an elite corporate training campus. Second, this training was our introduction to Six Sigma Black Belt—a set of statistical tools and techniques for process improvement. When I joined GE, the Six Sigma Black Belt certification was one of the most coveted stripes you could earn, and it was an essential element of our two-year executive management program. The training itself was pretty dry (read: boring AF), which was reflected in the intensity of our social evening team-building sessions (read: work hard, party harder).

During the first two days, I caught a few glimpses of Cara, which triggered and regenerated my considerable interest in getting to know her. I circled like a shark but found remarkably little opportunity.

The conference hotel was so large that our 150-strong gathering often split up into smaller groups that ventured outside the building. Since the training sessions were also split, I started to worry that once again, I would have no way to seek out Cara. Not that I wasn't having a good time—despite the fact that the daytime instruction was tedious, this training was actually much more fun than Crotonville. The group was made up of smart and ambitious go-getters who, for the most part, weren't shy about having a good time. As the week carried on, I went with the social flow, and the intriguing, pretty brunette drifted to the background of my imagination.

On the last evening, however, my luck changed in the best way possible.

After having dinner with a small group, we returned to the hotel, and some of us meandered into the bar, which we had basically closed down every night that week. We joined a group of familiar faces, and I was midsentence with one of my newfound GE buddies when I spotted Cara sitting at a high table toward the back of the bar. I felt a rush of excitement and immediately started plotting my move. I headed to the bar to order a beer, and when I turned around, I noticed out of the corner of my eye that Cara's companion had left the table.

I don't recall if the companion was a he or a she, or whether he or she went to get a drink, to dance, or to the bathroom, and frankly, I don't even remember if he or she came back. What I do know is that I beelined over to Cara's table, sat down, and launched into a conversation. Don't ask me what we talked about; I really don't remember. I do recall that when a waitress came by, I immediately offered to buy Cara a drink because I didn't want her to leave. She hesitated because she didn't want to make it a late night, but she finally agreed to a Coors Light. Defending her choice of beer, she said, "I'm a really cheap date."

She could have ordered a magnum of champagne, and I would have been perfectly fine with it. I was exactly where I wanted to be, sitting across from the beautiful girl who had first mesmerized me two months earlier.

Over the next few hours, my strategy was to keep ordering drinks and keep talking. And it worked. As the rounds of beer piled up, my overwhelming impression was how nice Cara was. Yes, the original attraction was most definitely physical, but she was a genuinely nice person, the kind of nice you simply cannot fake. She was down to earth and incredibly personable with no pretense whatsoever—almost a little naive, but in the best way possible.

During that first conversation, I learned that Cara was just twenty-four, had grown up in Pittsburgh, and attended Virginia Tech before joining GE Appliances in a sales rep program right out of college. I was thirty-one at the time, and although twenty-four seemed a little young, it was a trivial detail.

As the bar filled up with other people in the program, we eventually mingled into the crowd, but Cara had made an incredible impression on me. I knew I would want to get to know her better but had no clue how to really go from there.

The next morning, we were both a little tardy for the morning training session, so we bumped into each other getting coffee before sneaking in through the side door.

"I really enjoyed talking with you last night," I said, trying to remain cool and collected. "I hope we can do it again sometime."

Without any hesitation and with the cutest smile, she replied, "I'd like that. Just find me on Sametime."

Perhaps she was just being kind, but my overzealous male brain on the prowl registered the slightest hint of interest, and that was all I needed to hear. I was on cloud nine the rest of the day, elevated by the mere prospect that getting to know her better looked much more promising.

PING

Sametime was GE's internal prelude to instant messenger. Like the original AOL "You've got mail" pop-up, a Sametime text window appeared when someone tried to reach you, announcing itself with a distinct "ping."

The Monday morning following our Atlanta training, I was greeted with a ping that sent a bolt of electricity through me. It was Cara, sending a short message along the lines of "Hi, how are you?" This was definitely a good sign! That initial ping, and the few hours of Sametiming that followed, meant we had crossed the magical line from meeting to connecting.

Starting that Monday, our chats became daily. At first, it was just casual conversation about work, weekend adventures, or whatever might come up. Slowly, a little bit of flirtation entered into the chats, which became ever so slightly more personal. Toward late September, a little fluff of romance had entered the equation. Mind you; this was all by chat. We hadn't talked on the phone yet, and back then, texting wasn't as commonplace as it is now.

Then, sometime in early October, Cara called me late one night while she was at home in Pittsburgh. It was a drunk dial, with all sorts of noise (and girlfriends) in the background, and our chat wasn't meaningful or long, but it broke the ice on calling. I called her back the next day, and we took our long-distance flirting to the next level.

By now, it was obvious we both wanted to organize a date of some sort, but with 550 miles between us—Cara in Raleigh, North Carolina, and me in Stamford, Connecticut—doing so wasn't going to be easy. We discussed all sorts of possible weekend rendezvous scenarios, and then Cara mentioned she had never been to New York City for Christmas. NYC is a special place any time of the year, but at Christmas, it's magical. NYC was also my stomping grounds; I had lived there the previous eighteen months and still drove down from Stamford nearly every weekend to run around town with my business school buddies. So I invited Cara to come to NYC for a weekend so I could show her around the city while the Christmas decorations were in full force.

Cara flew in on Friday, December 13 (neither of us is very superstitious!), and took a cab into town. I met up with her at the lot where I had parked my car for the weekend, which was a few blocks from our hotel—the Envoy Club Suites on East Thirty-Third Street. We were both clearly excited to see each other, but the last time we actually met was in Atlanta, and we had only romanced digitally. What to do? We shared a warm hug, which broke the ice, and then we left to pick up some drinks and food for the hotel room and to check in and change for dinner.

As we went up to room 301 to change, there was a beautiful tension between us, the type of tension that results when you both know what's almost destined to happen, yet there's still the anticipation of it actually happening. Romance was in the air. When would it lead to that first kiss?

We met some of my friends for dinner that evening and had a great time, but we bailed on the after-party and charted our own way back toward the hotel. We somehow landed in a dive bar called Third & Long, just a few blocks from our hotel. Cara is from Pittsburgh, home of some excellent dive bars, so this choice was fine by her.

We bellied up to the bar, then swiveled our chairs to face each other, finally just the two of us, and sparks flew all over the place. We only had eyes for each other. The whole bar could have gone up in smoke, and we wouldn't have noticed.

While she went to the bathroom, I ordered another round of drinks. We locked eyes as she walked back to where we were sitting. Just before Cara climbed onto her bar chair, I gently pulled her toward me, and we kissed. Our first kiss. It was inevitable, and it was magic.

I don't recall how much longer we stayed in Third & Long. They probably didn't mind when we left. By that point, we were two smitten lovebirds at the bar, taking up valuable real estate and not ordering much.

We retreated to our hotel room and stayed up all night talking. Even though we shared the room and sparks flew all over the place, we somehow managed to keep things very innocent all weekend. It wasn't the time; we were just getting to know each other. We had an amazing weekend sightseeing and eating our way through the city, and by the time Sunday rolled around, we were both totally, and I mean totally, swept off our feet. Falling madly in love is such a beautiful thing.

DATING

The New York rendezvous broke the love levee, and our relationship moved into the fast and furious territory. We messaged and called daily and were soon aching to see each other again.

Cara spent Christmas with her family in Pittsburgh, and I was supposed to join my parents in Amsterdam, but a few projects forced me to stay in Stamford. I worked through Christmas and then trekked up to Vermont, where I had a share in a ski house for the winter season. I had a little over a week to ski and celebrate the New Year in the beautiful Vermont mountains before heading back to start my new rotation.

Right after Christmas, Cara and I started throwing around possible meetup dates for January. I think it was Cara who casually hinted she could also jump on a flight and join me in Vermont for New Year's. Two days later, on December 30, I picked her up from the Hartford airport, and we spent the next four days in a rickety, old, very cute ski chalet in snowy Vermont. There was nothing luxurious or opulent about this chalet, though it did have a few real fireplaces, and except for our rowdy New Year's Eve party, we had the whole place to ourselves. It was magical, and neither of us wanted to go back to reality.

I returned to Stamford, and Cara flew back to Pittsburgh and then onto Dallas, where she moved into a new apartment and prepared for her next rotation with GE. We immediately started planning another weekend date, which wasn't so easy to do since Dallas isn't exactly next door to Stamford. But given that Dallas is much warmer in the winter than Stamford, I usually flew to her in those early months of 2003, and like total foodies, we dated our way through the Dallas restaurant scene. The more time we spent together, the more our connection and affection deepened.

As every romantic relationship grows and evolves, it moves to new dimensions at different points in time. The catalyst might be an event, a conversation, or simply a glance or a touch, but there are moments when something changes or shifts in a significant and noticeable way. Sometime in late February or early March, Cara visited me up north for another weekend in New York City, and we had one such moment.

It was midevening on Saturday. After a fun day of exploring the city, we had dinner with some of my friends, and afterward, we broke away for a nightcap. We settled in with some drinks in a swanky cocktail lounge that was only just starting to come alive. Suddenly, Cara took on a much more serious look and told me she wanted to share something with me. I didn't think too much of it, so I quipped some fast line, but she said she really wanted to talk to me. At that point, she had my attention; something was clearly weighing on her.

Cara proceeded to share that she knew that on the weekends we didn't meet up, I was mostly engulfed in the NYC nightlife with my friends—and she could only imagine what that entailed.

"I'm not the kind of girl who wants to play," she said. "I want something more serious. If that isn't mutual, I don't know if I want to continue. I'm starting to have really strong feelings for you, and I need to know if you see things the same way. I want our relationship to be exclusive."

As she spoke, Cara couldn't have looked any more beautiful, so vulnerable and exposed yet incredibly poised and elegant in her delivery.

"I understand if this isn't what you want," she continued, "but I need you to be honest with me. I'm really falling in love with you."

At first, I didn't know what to say. I understood what she was sharing with me. It perfectly fit her personality and the type of girl she was—hell, it was exactly what you want a girl you're serious about to say. But this was also a major milestone in our young relationship. When you agree to go "exclusive," you cross a magical threshold, and the significance of this moment was instantly apparent to me. It wasn't so much that I was being requested to curtail my extracurricular activities on the other weekends; for me, the significance was more the positive decision to fully commit—to go all in—to my relationship with Cara. It had been only nine months since my divorce had been finalized, and although my ex-wife wasn't even remotely in the picture, I had come to enjoy a certain freedom, and I had not set out to rush into another serious relationship.

Even though all these thoughts raced through my mind, it was ultimately only a split second before I confirmed that I wanted the same thing. I was absolutely crazy about Cara, and there was no doubt in my mind that I wanted to see us take things to the next level. I got a kick out of the fact that this beautiful twenty-five-year-old just told this thirty-one-year-old to step up to the plate. Surely, we would have gotten to this point organically, but her prompting led to a mutual expression of our intentions and feelings. It became a watershed moment that confirmed that our growing love and affection was shared, not just in experience but in where we wanted to go with it. It allowed us to enter a new dimension of our young relationship, and it cleared the path of acceleration that followed. I absolutely love that she put me on the spot that evening; it was a beautiful moment.

Over the next few months, with Cara still living in Dallas and me in Stamford, we continued our long-distance love affair by planning fun weekend escapades and meetups, with a few more noteworthy milestone events thrown in: a weekend in Pittsburgh to meet her parents for the first time and a ski trip to Colorado to meet mine.

As we approached the end of our current rotations, the question emerged of what to do next. We each would have options, and possibly the best rotations for both of us would mean continuing to date long-distance. Conversely, we could each choose our next rotation around geography, but that might mean one or both of us having to sacrifice professionally.

At first, we scooted around the topic, but as the selection dates neared, our conversations became more serious, and it was obvious that both of us wanted to live in close proximity to each other. It wasn't a major leap from there to agree we would both go for rotations in south Connecticut since that area offered both of us the most options.

I was only a year into being at GE Capital, and some colleagues and friends expressed concern about my decision to not necessarily optimize my rotation selection (and prioritize my career) over this relatively new relationship. I realize now that in choosing love, I clearly got it right this time, although unfortunately, that wasn't always the case before or after. Career, work, and professional fulfillment are all important, but I learned the hard way that they shouldn't trump the maybe handful of chances you get at experiencing real love and connection in your life.

Being the quintessential alpha male go-getter, my ego completely identified with career, money, power, and achievement. There was always a next level to chase and conquer; that carousel never stops. In my relationship with Cara, as with others, I inevitably started investing disproportionate time and effort into my professional endeavors. The girl gets into the chariot because she's been promised a beautiful journey, but I somehow got lost in buying her the most beautiful chariot in the world, not realizing all she really wanted from me was the journey.

More on this later; let's continue the fairy tale for now.

MOVING IN

The rotation selection process was interesting. Imagine all sorts of "jobs" posted by different business units with role descriptions and associated assignment leaders. Add to that smorgasbord of options our mutually imposed proximity location constraints, and we were looking at rotations mostly in Stamford, Norwalk, and Danbury, Connecticut. We ended up doing pretty well, with me moving to another business in Stamford and Cara joining a business unit in Danbury about thirty minutes away.

With that settled, Cara needed to sort out her new housing, and as fate (or luck!) would have it, my lease was coming up for renewal, and my roommate was moving out, so I was planning to move as well. It was one thing to doctor our rotations so we could be in the general proximity of each other, but now a whole new topic slipped into the conversation: Where is she going to live, where am I going to live, and what if we actually lived together?

Moving in together is another one of those milestone events in a relationship where things shift to a higher gear and the next level of commitment. We sort of backed into the topic by first talking around it, endlessly evaluating where we would each ideally have our apartments, which naturally evolved into the discussion of how much time she would spend at my place or vice versa. As we strategically analyzed our options from all angles (as good corporate minions should do), the only logical conclusion was that we needed to live close—in the same town. Of course, we were just talking around the elephant in the room, each of us a little shy about fully expressing what we really wanted.

The program included reimbursement for a house-hunting trip for Cara, so we planned a fun weekend escape to drive around Fairfield County, Connecticut, and figure out all our housing options while having romantic dinners and exploring the stunning countryside. Situated in the foothills of the Berkshire Mountains, this part of the country, especially in early summer with everything in bloom, is absolutely beautiful: soft, rolling hills with lush tree cover and lots of lakes and reservoirs.

We cruised along the long, winding country roads that connect Danbury and Stamford, through classic New England hamlets like New Canaan, Wilton, Weston, and Ridgefield, and the moment we drove into Ridgefield, we were both sold. Ridgefield split the commute, with Cara being fifteen minutes from her new office location and me being about twenty to twenty-five minutes from Stamford. Ridgefield is a 300-year-old quaint township tucked away in the sloping countryside of Fairfield County, with gorgeous colonial-style houses and a charming old main street. It's the quintessential New England village. Of course, it's also a sleepy little place with only twenty-five thousand residents and little to no major offices or industry, so there wasn't much in terms of apartment housing. As a result, our house hunting quickly became just that—*house* hunting.

Although the living-together option remained unspoken, we only found and looked at rental properties we would have to share. At this point, gravity prevailed, and over dinner, we finally addressed the topic head-on. It was a classic moment, where the combination of relief and excitement dissipates the nervous energy of wondering whether what you want is shared by the other person. In this case, the desire was definitely mutual. We were both madly in love, and that weekend, we stepped into the possibility of finding a rental house in Ridgefield and moving in together.

Or so I thought. The house-hunting weekend was successful in that we found where we wanted to live (Ridgefield) and how we wanted to live (together), but we still had some searching to do. We found some okay options, but nothing we were crazy about.

Being thirty-one and divorced already, I also didn't fully appreciate that for Cara, moving in together was a huge step—something she wanted to make sure her parents were okay with. I was eighteen when I left home to attend college in Amsterdam and twenty-one when I left my home country, so the notion of asking my parents didn't even occur to me. Being seven years younger than me, being a daughter, and having grown up in a more traditional Catholic family, Cara approached the situation quite differently.

I distinctly remember being in a supermarket when Cara called, totally exuberant. "I told her, and she said yes!"

Puzzled and somewhat confused, I asked, "Who did you tell what, and what exactly did she say yes to?"

"My mom said yes. We can totally live together. She was okay with it!"

I cracked up and told Cara I didn't know that our living together was subject to her mom's approval, but I was happy to hear we could move forward.

What Cara actually told her mom was that it was really expensive to rent and that it would be more economical as well as practical if we were roommates because we would be spending all of our time together anyway. Her mom was no fool, and she knew exactly what was going on: we were two kids in love who wanted to live together.

With the path now officially cleared, I started making real work of finding a place, and a dozen or so houses later, I found our dream home: a little two-story, two-bedroom red cottage with its own separate driveway and large lawn. It was part of a much larger estate that was located just up a small hill, where our landlords— the cutest retired couple—lived.

The cottage was very old, with vintage oak floors and a small, dated kitchen with a 1970s feel. It had a musty basement with storage and an old washer and dryer, two smallish upstairs bedrooms, and a tiny upstairs bathroom. For the next year, I took crooked showers because the slanted roof prevented me from standing up straight. We didn't care one bit. It was a perfect romantic cottage, and we happily signed the lease and moved in.

We didn't simply move in; we also opened a joint bank account. Even though I made quite a bit more than Cara, I suggested we share an account and pay our bills from that. I don't care much for fussing about who pays for what or keeping track of who paid what bill. More importantly, it seems to me that you allow a certain energy to flow when you opt to go all in. When there's holding back, reservations, and safety precautions, then there's really lack of commitment (and no energy flow!). For any relationship to have any real chance of succeeding, I am convinced there needs to be a 100 percent wholehearted decision to make the relationship succeed. Maybe six months is a little early to make this decision, but when you know, you just know. And if you have such fundamental differences in habits or values around money that you can't blindly trust your partner as you would trust yourself, you might have to evaluate your compatibility. After all, love and compatibility aren't necessarily the same thing; you need lots of both to make it work over the long-term. Cara totally agreed, and we never looked back. I can honestly say we never had one discussion about it afterward. Sharing our money and expenses was natural for both of us, so we simply flowed with it.

I have nothing but good memories of Ridgefield and our time in that cute little place. Our rotations went well, our commutes were manageable, and our weekends were spectacular and fun. We hiked, worked out, moseyed around Main Street, went shopping in White Plains, made day trips to New York City, ventured up to Rhode Island (Narragansett and Newport were our favorites), or hung out in our little cottage on snowy winter days, watching movies and cooking great food. Our romance was humming on all cylinders, and life was good.

About halfway through our one-year lease, the time came for the fourth and final rotation in our executive management training program. This was a pivotal career moment for both of us because the fourth rotation—which was decided by a quasi-draft from the businesses where you had a rotation before—determined which business you would join when that final rotation ended.

Cara was fortunate to be drafted into the GE Consumer Finance division, which had its headquarters in Stamford. I was fortunate to have the choice of going to any of my previous business units and decided on GE Capital Aviation Services (GECAS), which was also in Stamford. However, my new role at GECAS slowly but surely required more travel, which meant many trips to JFK or LaGuardia Airport—a bit of a trek from Ridgefield. As much as we loved Ridgefield, it became obvious that being closer to Stamford would be more practical for both of us.

Toward the end of our lease, we started looking for places in and around Stamford. With a background in real estate, I gravitated toward buying something versus continuing to rent, and although we weren't even engaged at this stage (I don't think that topic had even entered the conversation yet), we both seemed to think buying a house together made all the sense in the world.

We went on house-hunting trips and found a new eight-unit townhouse development in Stamford, less than five minutes from our respective offices and close to everything. We moved in around May 2004, eighteen months after our first date in NYC, and about a month shy of starting our new jobs at GE. It was all smooth sailing on the career side, and with our double income and no-kids lifestyle, we were able to furnish our new little love nest to our heart's content. We settled into Stamford for the next chapter of our relationship.

Life has this special zest about it when you have love in your life. Everything is amplified, colors are brighter, scents are stronger, feelings are deeper, and your heart opens up so the vibrancy of life itself can feed and nourish your very being. That's where we were, with the beauty of life dancing in the palms of our hands.

GETTING SERIOUS

As we settled into our new jobs and our new house in Stamford, our destiny to marry and be together became almost inevitable. My first marriage and divorce had long faded into the rearview mirror, and although I was not in any rush to get back to the wedding altar, I wasn't in any way hesitant about it with Cara. If nothing else, I knew what it meant for her, and because of that, marriage came into focus for me during the summer of 2004.

Like we had done the previous two years, that Labor Day weekend, we visited the US Open tennis tournament at Flushing Meadows in New York. Typically, we arrived late afternoon and roamed the grounds a bit before scoring some dinner. Then, a few beers in hand (Cara still liked her Coors Light), we settled into our seats to enjoy the night matches.

That weekend, sitting high up in the bleachers with my arm around Cara, I peered up into the perfectly clear sky covered with stars. I looked over at Cara, and she was fully engulfed in the tennis match, following it intently with her half-finished beer in one hand while she leaned slightly forward with her legs crossed. A gentle breeze played ever so softly with her beautiful brown hair.

I looked at her, up to the sky, and back at her, and it hit me: she was the one for me. It was time. I loved her with all my heart; she was everything I wanted and needed. Whatever shred of residual doubt there might have been, that evening, it evaporated into the beautiful star-filled sky above Flushing Meadows.

It was early September, and I had work to do. I wanted to create something magical, something so memorable that it would be engraved in our memories forever. Mapping out the timeline and things to do—planning when to ask for her hand in marriage, finding an engagement ring, and organizing a special place and evening—was both exhilarating and challenging. By now, I traveled all the time, and living together made it hard to keep things under wraps.

Balancing all these things put my target date somewhere in December, which triggered the idea to recreate our very first date. *Boom!* Now I had a date to work toward: December 13. With that in mind, I called the Envoy Club Suites to see about rebooking room 301, the exact room where we originally stayed in 2002. The problem with this hotel is that it primarily caters to long-term stays by executives and only rents out its open rooms if and when available. Some of these executives stay for weeks or even months at a time, so there was no way for the hotel to guarantee the room I would be assigned.

I am a persistent guy when I know what I want, and in this case, I was relentless. I escalated the conversation to the hotel manager, whom I came to know on a first-name basis. I even drove down from Stamford once to make a personal plea. I figured maybe, just maybe, she would respond to my all-out attempts to make this a really special night for my bride to be. I never received any guarantees, but somehow (and I don't believe it was a coincidence) on the morning we were to check in, I would learn that they had reserved room 301 for us and made all the necessary preparations—and not just the flowers, candles, chocolates, and champagne I had coordinated with them. They would double down on everything, compliments of the hotel.

That fall, we traveled to Pittsburgh to visit her parents, and I collaborated with Cara's mom to have her whisked away for some shopping while I asked for her hand in marriage. Cara's dad is a gastroenterologist with a brilliant mind. He loves to play golf and have a good time, but he's a man of few words. Our conversation was brief and matter of fact. After he said he would be delighted to see us get married, we went back to watching the ball game on TV without mincing another word on the subject.

Internally, I breathed a sigh of relief. Deep down, I knew that having been married before must be a blemish on my credentials for devout Catholics like Cara's parents. They never expressed that to me, never gave me so much as an inkling that my divorce played any factor for them, and for that, I have always been immensely thankful. I was welcomed into Cara's family, both direct and extended, with the warmest embrace you could imagine. She's from a truly special family, and I have nothing but love and admiration for them.

With her father's blessing secured, all arrangements in place, and the ring purchased, the path was clear for our two-year-anniversary date. The days leading up to the weekend, I had a little nervous pit in my stomach, not because I doubted she would say yes, but because I wanted it to be special and memorable. I readily admit I am a hopeless romantic at heart, but since life is really just a string of moments and memories, creating *special* moments and *meaningful* memories seems only natural and important.

The day I proposed to Cara, December 13, 2004—exactly two years to the day of our first date in the very same hotel room—is mostly a blur until the time we returned from dinner. As we came into the room, I led Cara to the bench in front of the bed and asked her to take a seat. I suspect she had a feeling all along, but as I bent down to one knee and took her hand in mine, there was no doubt what was happening. I detected a small tear of joy and expectancy as our eyes locked. Mutual excitement and anticipation filled the air. This moment was electric.

Proposing to someone does strange things to time. It's a brief moment that feels like the very longest. After I shared my carefully rehearsed words with a little bit of a tremor in my voice, I asked, "Will you marry me?" while looking up into her eyes.

Her face lit up, and she lovingly mumbled, "Yes, of course, I will."

Everything about that moment—the look in her eyes, those words, and the feeling of sheer joy and shared excitement about our future together—is so precious to me. It left an indelible mark on my heart, like a smoldering hot iron, never to be the same again.

Like the previous years, we spent Christmas with Cara's family and had even more fun than usual. We showed up filled with excitement about our engagement ten days earlier only to meet up with her extended family and find they were practically as happy as we were. This was a Christmas for the ages.

We rolled into 2005 on an incredible high, with work-life going as well as our personal life. Cara was thriving, and I started climbing the corporate ladder at an accelerated pace. In many ways, GECAS was the perfect fit for me within the larger corporate behemoth. My business unit was one of the leading aircraft leasing companies in the world, with over 1,500 aircraft in its portfolio and more than $55 billion in assets. Not only was my business unit very profitable, but it "only" had three hundred employees worldwide and was quite strategic to GE because the manufacturing side produced aircraft engines. Being in a boutique business with relatively few employees meant there weren't many layers of management, and fairly early on, I had direct exposure to the top executives—exposure I may not have had until years later in other units.

In this business, there are only two types of people on the front lines (i.e., the sales side): *metal* or *finance*. I was never going to be a metal guy since I had no specific background or pedigree in aviation or aircraft, but I realized early on that I could be a finance guy because I've always had a knack for numbers. So in my fourth rotation, I went on a training binge to become the best damn pricing guy in GECAS. I volunteered to do everyone's pricing (because practice makes perfect), and while others thought I had lost my mind, this decision paid huge dividends later on. I became really good, really fast at very complicated aircraft leasing pricing. The second-highest executive in GECAS was a "quant jock"—a wizard with numbers—and my skills caught his attention. From that moment on, my career took off, my paychecks grew exponentially, and at age thirty-five, I became the first from my executive management program class to make executive band in GE, which roughly translates to the top 1 percent of the company.

With my growing responsibilities and paycheck also came more pressure and time constraints. I was now traveling globally on a regular basis, flying to China one week and Brazil the next. Right around the time Cara and I got engaged and started planning our wedding, my GE career started accelerating. I was running on rocket fuel.

Nevertheless, all parts of our life were exciting. We were flying high at full throttle, so we dove in headfirst to figure out our wedding in those early months of 2005.

WEDDING BELLS AND MORE

We briefly considered a wedding in Pittsburgh, but neither Cara nor I wanted to have a traditional wedding. One thing I learned from my first wedding is that I only wanted to invite people we actually knew. The first time around, my in-laws invited all sorts of extended family—some my wife didn't even remember meeting. Cara's dad was a prominent physician and longtime country club member, so getting married in Pittsburgh would mean lots of people I didn't know and would probably never see again. Additionally, I wasn't Catholic, so a Pittsburgh wedding would bring that awkward dilemma to the surface.

With both our careers going full speed and limited time to spend on planning, we quickly realized that a destination wedding might have several advantages. Once you pick a destination and make arrangements, you leave the rest of the fretting to the wedding planner. In addition, you can more easily keep the invitation list short and sweet.

I have a friend from business school in the hospitality business, and among a few other places in the Caribbean, he suggested we check out Playa del Carmen. We arranged a wedding site scouting trip that spring and fell in love with the place. Playa del Carmen is a sleepy little beach town with a ton of Mexican charm. It's also close to Cancún, which is easily accessible from Amsterdam, as well as anywhere in the United States.

My friend also arranged for us to meet with a local boutique hotel called the Blue Parrot Hotel, an institution in Playa del Carmen located directly on the beach. Just weeks before, the Blue Parrot had hired a wedding planner to help the hotel get more seriously into the destination wedding business, so they were eager to work with us. Still, nailing down the date turned out to be a challenge, as the hotel was booked up months ahead of time. To block the whole hotel, we had to stretch the date into 2006. We settled on February 18, 2006, which coincided with Presidents' Day weekend, giving people a great excuse to come join us in the sun for our wedding.

Then we learned that Mexican law required our blood to be drawn by a government official, and marriage papers from Mexico tended to have errors and not be recognized in the United States. This quandary led us to rethink our plans a bit. We decided to get married in the States first so we would have an official marriage certificate, and then enjoy a Playa del Carmen ceremonial wedding.

And that's how we ended up getting married in Las Vegas by none other than Elvis Presley! I've always been a huge Elvis fan, so I was all over this idea. Cara, in all her practicality, was a great sport and, after taking a couple deep breaths, went right along with my plan. This also provided the opportunity for our parents to meet before the wedding in Mexico. We invited them all to join us for a long weekend in Las Vegas, where we were married on November 4, 2005. Our Elvis-themed wedding became a fantastic weekend visiting shows, eating at excellent restaurants, and lounging by the pool. The six of us had a blast!

A gorgeous wedding calls for an epic honeymoon, and with the wedding planning pretty much on cruise control, we started to look into our options there. We both managed to get approval to roll some vacation time into 2006, so we could take almost three weeks off for our honeymoon. We tossed around ideas like New Zealand and India, then landed on a safari in South Africa. We ended up tagging on a visit to Victoria Falls in Zambia, as well.

We had so much to look forward to as we closed out 2005. After the holidays, our excitement grew by the day. Before we could make it to the altar, however, we had to fight the weather gods in the Northeast.

We were scheduled to leave for Playa del Carmen on the Monday morning before our Saturday wedding. Most of our guests were arriving a few days early, and we planned to complete our final arrangements in the early part of the week so we could party with our friends and family as they trickled in. But a massive cold front with serious snowfall moved in the weekend before we left, throwing a major wrench into our plans.

On Sunday, we drove through the snow to New Jersey so we could stay with Cara's aunt and uncle in preparation for our early morning flight from Newark. First thing the next morning, her uncle drove us to the airport. It's not a good sign when you can't see the road because of the snow, and even worse when you can't see the guard rails. To this day, I have no idea how her uncle managed to get us to the airport and then back home safely.

Seriously worried that our flight would be canceled, we were pleasantly surprised that we could actually check in. The weather looked ominous, but the flight boarded right on time, and Cara and I felt we had dodged a huge bullet. Then came the announcement, and sitting in our seats ready to take off, our hearts stopped. All we wanted to do was get to Playa del Carmen, and there we were, stranded at Newark in an epic snowstorm.

After we deboarded, I beelined it to the ticket counter to figure out our alternatives while Cara retrieved our bags. There were no flight alternatives out of Newark until Thursday, but because of my elite status (all of that global travel came in handy!), I managed to get us on another flight out of JFK the very next day, which then meant we somehow had to get to JFK. The snowstorm had shut down the bus services, but I was still able to get a rental car, and we managed to make it to an airport hotel at JFK around lunchtime.

The snowstorm didn't let up, however, and by early evening, our worst fears were confirmed: our morning flight was canceled. With no alternative flights from the NY area available for days to come, we had a real problem on our hands. Cara had held up really well so far, but at this point, she burst into tears. I wasn't far behind her, to be honest, but I pulled myself together and called an airline representative. I explained that we hadn't simply missed our flight; we missed the flight to our wedding. We started running through all possible options to get us down to Cancún. Turns out, the representative had two seats left on an early morning flight out of Washington, DC. Without having the faintest idea of how we would make it there, I told her to book the seats.

When I hung up, I looked at Cara and said, "Don't worry. I got us on a flight to Cancún tomorrow morning. We're going to be in Playa del Carmen tomorrow by noon."

She cracked a shy smile, somewhat relieved to hear I was so confident that we were going to be in Playa del Carmen tomorrow, but also wondered how we were going to make it to DC by the next morning in the middle of a raging snowstorm.

"Don't worry," I said again. "We'll rent a car. I don't mind driving in the snow. I'm from Holland, and we do that all time."

She looked at me and said, "You're so full of shit. You guys don't have any snow in Holland; you only have rain!" Then she burst out laughing and added, "You're totally nuts. Who on earth drives to Washington in a storm like this? This is exactly why I am marrying you on Saturday."

The ice was broken, and her spirits were back. We were going to be in Playa del Carmen the next day, come hell or high water.

It wasn't easy to find a rental car. By then, it was late on Monday, and most places were closed due to the storm. Cara's sister lives in Washington, DC, though, so if we could make it there that night, we had a place to crash for a few hours before we had to catch our flight.

We managed to navigate the rental companies and the snowstorm, make it to Washington that night, and arrive in Playa del Carmen by noon on Tuesday, just as promised—only to be met by our next challenge.

Our wedding planner, Paula, had arranged for our transfer from the Cancún airport to Playa del Carmen, and we were a little surprised she came with the driver to pick us up. As we made the hour-long drive from the airport to Playa del Carmen, we found out why. A few days before, there had been a little accident during the nightly fire show, and the palapa—a tiki hut and *our wedding venue*—had caught fire. She wanted to assure us that they were already making the necessary repairs and that our wedding was going to be just fine.

When we arrived, the driver took care of our bags, and Paula led us toward the bar and lounge area, which was located right behind the reception area.

As I turned the corner, my jaw dropped—there was absolutely nothing left of the bar and lounge. It had literally burned down to the ground; all that remained were the charred stumps of the original wooden support columns. Aside from a few day laborers who were tidying up, there was no evidence whatsoever of rebuilding—no building materials, no tools or ladders, no construction workers anywhere in sight.

It didn't take a real estate development background to see that this venue wasn't going to be back up in three days. I looked over at Cara. Tears streamed down her cheeks as she took in the sorry ruins where her wedding was to take place in just a few days. Most girls dream about a few things their whole life, and a picture-perfect wedding is one of them. Cara was no different. She stood there staring at the ruins, still reeling from the snowstorm and our flight saga, no longer able to stop her tears. I gave her a big hug, kissed her forehead, and whispered that it was going to be just fine. I had no idea how or what to do, but it broke my heart to see her like this, and all I wanted to do was make it better.

Over the years, I've noticed a peculiar dynamic between men and women. In a time of crisis or despair, all women really want to know from men is that it's going to be okay. They don't need all the details, and men don't even need to have a plan; women simply want to see men keep their cool and hear them say it's going to be okay. I didn't have a clue on how to solve this yet but seeing me stay calm and collected helped Cara come around, and her tears slowly dried. We walked back to Paula and calmly shared we needed to start working on an alternative plan because we didn't have much confidence in this venue coming back before Saturday. The strength and resilience I saw in Cara were intoxicating. It validated how much I admired and loved her. I couldn't wait for Saturday so she could become my wife before the whole world.

The owners of the Blue Parrot readily acknowledged nothing would be rebuilt by Saturday. In its place, they offered to rent a giant tent and place it on the beach right in front of the dance floor. That was even better than our original plan! Most of our guests never knew about our wedding venue drama because by the time Thursday came around, the wedding tent was erected on the beach, ready for our ceremony.

The rest of the wedding week was spectacular. Surrounded by

all our dearest friends and family, we ate, drank, laughed, and partied day and night. Our wedding day itself was perhaps even more magical than I could have ever imagined. We exchanged vows on the beach about an hour before sunset, right in front of the boutique hotel we had fully reserved. Chairs were set up on either side of the center aisle, which was covered with flower petals. Cara looked radiant in her glamorous, floor-length wedding dress with her hair pinned up.

Some images become embedded in your memory as if carved into bedrock, and Cara on our wedding day is one of those images for me. She looked stunning.

After the ceremony, we enjoyed an incredible dinner and epic party in the beautifully decorated beach tent. Later on, we pretty much closed down Playa del Carmen together with the wedding guests who joined us for the after-party—about half of the hundred or so who came. It was deep into the night when Cara and I made it back to our wedding suite at the Blue Parrot Hotel. We had an unforgettable wedding, and our future together couldn't look any brighter.

Six weeks later, we took off for our honeymoon, sparing no expense: we traveled business class to and from South Africa, lined up some of the finest hotels, and arranged for every possible sightseeing trip of any interest.

We landed in Cape Town, where we toured the city as well as Franschhoek, better known as South African wine country. We visited Robben Island, the prisoner camp where Nelson Mandela was held for close to twenty-seven years. Seeing his living conditions and learning more about his circumstances left a deep impression on us and became the most memorable part of Cape Town. Next, we visited the Mala Mala Game Reserve in Kruger National Park and saw South African wildlife up close in an experience for the ages. The final stage of our grand honeymoon was a visit to Victoria Falls on the border of Zambia and Zimbabwe. We stayed in a beautiful luxury boutique resort with cottages overlooking the Zambezi River. The riverside of our idyllic cottage was completely open, covered only by a mosquito net, and so it felt like we were sleeping in the jungle. We toured Victoria Falls—rightfully considered one of the seven natural wonders of the world—went white water rafting, and took sunset cruises on the Zambezi River, all followed by long dinners and late nights around campfires, peering into the starlit skies of Zambia.

All good things must come to an end, and as we prepared to make our long trip back home, I felt grateful and happy. We were beyond crazy in love, and life was good.

Really, really good.

PART II

REAL LIFE

The darkest nights produce the brightest stars.

—JOHN GREEN

UPWARD AND ONWARD

Freshly married and back from our fabulous honeymoon, Cara and I both returned to fast-tracked careers and rising paychecks. I was fortunate to be part of a highly profitable business unit known for paying its top performers very well. With great performance reviews, my bonuses were becoming quite substantial, and we enjoyed an entirely carefree lifestyle outside work.

With the escalating pay came increased work pressure, and for me, that meant traveling two to three weeks out of the month, often to far corners of the world. By nature, I am a deal junkie, and my job involved working on major aircraft leasing deals worth tens if not hundreds of millions of dollars. We were wheeling and dealing commercial aircraft like they were Mattel toy cars. Being this closely involved with big business was a major adrenaline rush that immediately hooked me.

In late summer of 2006, I was promoted to the newly formed airport infrastructure group, a perfect fit with my real estate development background. My new boss was located in London, and the day after my promotion, I flew to England because they were already negotiating an acquisition.

Careers in corporate behemoths like GE are ultimately determined by a few key pivot points, usually only traceable in hindsight, and this promotion was one of those points. In this highly visible position in a new highly visible growth initiative, I had to show up, deliver, and be good to succeed (in work and life). I also needed a healthy dose of fortitude. This acceleration of my career only fueled my competitive nature and drive to succeed, excel, and go faster and further up the corporate food chain.

Like the frog that slowly boils to death in gradually heated water, increasing stress and work pressures slowly heated the pot of my life. Inevitably, life became less carefree, but we were still very much connected on every level. It helped that we worked for the same company and spoke the same corporate language. Although we saw much less of each other during the week due to my travel schedule, we enjoyed our weekends and vacations, which reinforced our connectedness.

As we settled into life in our Stamford townhouse, we also settled into some simple routines that nurtured our relationship. I treasured these mundane experiences, my favorite being our lazy Sunday mornings. With classical music playing in the background, we'd make a fancy breakfast and lounge in our pj's, with Cara reading her favorite magazines and me dissecting the Sunday *New York Times*. These few hours were a sacred block of time of simply being together.

We also took day trips to New York City, moseyed around the mall in White Plains, ate out, or caught a movie. These weekend excursions weren't anything spectacular, but quality time experiencing life together fostered so much closeness and connectedness, despite our increasingly hectic and disjointed weekdays.

We also dreamed out loud about having a family one day, what we wanted our life to look like in the future, and where we wanted to live. Although our careers were going very well, neither of us felt the Northeast was our home. As beautiful and opulently wealthy as the area is, there's also a certain harshness to it, in both the climate and the prevailing outlook on life. The financial sector is calculated, cold, and merciless. It's a dog-eat-dog world, and that mentality is seen in the wealthy enclaves where people directly and indirectly tied to this sector live. In general, people are more terse and abrupt, and they lack some of the friendliness and gentility found in other parts of the country.

That didn't mesh well with the true nature of a western Pennsylvania girl like Cara, or me for that matter. We also longed to live in a warmer climate and in a place with a free spirit and lots of outdoor splendor. We loved our visits to Colorado and the West in general, so as we daydreamed about where we would want to live next, we made a shortlist of five cities that met all our criteria: San Diego, Portland, Seattle, Denver, and Austin. Daydreaming together and plotting out our future reinforced our sense of being on this journey together as a couple.

In my experience, serendipity shows up by invitation. By taking small steps toward your goals and objectives, you invite chance to lend you a hand. That's exactly how we ended up living in Austin.

As GE looked to expand its airport platform, one of my main tasks was to find companies we could acquire or invest in, thus bolstering our capabilities and reach in the marketplace. One such target company was a Houston-based firm that specialized in developing on-airport real estate. We negotiated for close to eight months, and by early 2007, we secured the acquisition through GE Capital's arduous credit approval system.

I still remember sitting in the cavernous conference room at the fancy law firm, my boss from London sitting next to me, the owner flanked by his legal team sitting across from us. We were there to sign the final contract—but instead, the owner explained he wanted to pull out of the deal. There was nothing we could do to convince him otherwise, and countless hours and months of hard work disappeared down the drain.

Deflated, disillusioned, and bitterly disappointed, my boss and I quietly walked out of the conference room. "This is not good," my boss said wryly. "What the fuck do we do now?"

Only half-joking, I said, "Let's drive to Austin. There's a competitor firm there, and we'll just buy that company instead."

I wasn't full of bull here. During the underwriting process with the Houston firm, I had traveled throughout the country to meet all the major competitors in the space. I had met the owner in Austin a few months before and had no doubt he would accept another meeting. I didn't know if he was open to selling his company or to partnering with us, but we would cross that bridge when we got there.

"Are you serious?" my boss asked.

"Serious as a heart attack," I replied. "Let me make a call."

A few hours later, we were having dinner with the owner in Austin, and less than four months after that, we closed on the acquisition of a 50 percent interest in his company.

During the acquisition process, I formulated the post-acquisition business plan, so I had a free hand in creating the proposed management structure, as well as how we would grow the business and integrate it into GECAS. A few months into this process, I asked Cara how she felt about moving to Austin. She was a bit surprised, but when I explained I had the opportunity to carve out a leadership role for myself in this Austin-based firm, she quickly became excited.

Because my move to Austin was for GE, Cara was able to negotiate working remotely from Austin, so she didn't have to sacrifice her career. Moreover, we had an even bigger and more exciting change on the way: Cara was expecting and due to deliver in December of that year.

In May 2007, we bought a newly constructed house in Austin, a block from the running trail surrounding Lake Lady Bird, a few blocks from South Congress Avenue (a popular Austin hotspot), and right across the Colorado River from downtown Austin. I started my exciting new executive leadership role in the newly acquired firm, and we looked forward to the birth of our first child. Our fairy tale just kept getting better.

* * *

Everything in life comes at a price, and my new position was no exception. My already heavy travel schedule became incrementally more taxing as we started pursuing a large-scale development project in Moscow (Russia), as well as a major portfolio acquisition in Stockholm (Sweden), and several other projects in far-flung places like Bogotá (Colombia) and Dalian (China). We were hunting metaphorical elephants, and with my increasing responsibilities, the pressure to win deals became palpable.

We closed on the Stockholm portfolio acquisition in late 2007, which temporarily provided some breathing room. At the same time, I was asked to become GE's representative on the board of this company. I loved the deal, and Stockholm is a spectacular city, but it was a new responsibility added to my already full workload and travel schedule.

On top of that, our megadevelopment deal in Moscow wasn't tracking so well, and with close to $1 million in deal costs racked up already, pressure was mounting to pull this deal out of the fire. Traveling to Moscow from Austin is like going to the far ends of the earth, but nothing is as grueling as trying to negotiate a sophisticated business deal with a group of unscrupulous white-collar Russian business elite whose main objective is to abuse their power and force their way through intimidation tactics.

As 2007 rolled into 2008, I was living in two vastly different worlds. On the one hand, I had a wholesome and serene home life—a new baby, a gorgeous wife, a dream home in a fantastic city. On the other hand, I lived inside a relentless corporate pressure cooker with a nauseating travel schedule and incessant demands to deliver results yesterday. One day, I was bathing my newborn, and twenty-four hours later, I was across the globe in a marathon negotiating session with wealthy, untrustworthy, deceitful, and largely scum-of-the-earth suits. From my baby's nursery to a smoke-filled room with machine-gun-toting bodyguards standing in the corner. It was surreal at times, and I found it increasingly challenging to make sense of the dichotomy between my home and work life.

From a career perspective, I was still cooking with gas. I was recognized once again as a top performer, for which I received a massive bonus, and more importantly, I was nominated to attend GE's venerable manager development course (MDC). MDC was a major recognition in GE, reserved for those who were being groomed as the next top brass. My career was clearly on solid footing.

When Sam was born, Cara took maternity leave, followed by an extended leave of absence. As she settled into motherhood and life in Austin, her interest to return to GE waned. She knew the inevitable fate of her career trajectory if she were to become a part-timer working remotely. She ultimately decided not to return to GE, partly because my mounting workload and travel schedule meant I was often of little help with Sam and partly because my new income meant she didn't need to work.

And so, ever so gradually, our lives—which had been so intertwined on so many levels—started to diverge. It was a long time before we recognized these apparently innocuous and perfectly natural changes, but like running water carves a canyon over time, the eroding forces in our relationship were undeniably set in motion.

As my work and career became more serious, a certain gravity seeped into my being. Life simply wasn't as carefree anymore, and although I didn't fully appreciate it at the time, I now understand how the pressure to produce started to have its effect on me. The happy-go-lucky Robert became more staid, reserved, and withdrawn, and the direct exposure to the underbelly of big business left me increasingly jaded. I became tougher, more cynical, more calculated, and more cold-blooded, as those were the traits I needed to succeed in the world of big business and high finance. Looking back, I have no doubt that Cara found this Robert harder to connect with—not on purpose, not by design, but by mere circumstance.

Some of the burden was entirely self-imposed. A prisoner of my own ambition, I always strove harder than I was asked to, always pushed for more and better when everyone else had long been satisfied. The relentless drive and insatiable need to prove my worth that got me ahead eventually became the thing that brought me down.

AN EPIC CRISIS

In the early months of 2008, it was already evident in GE Capital that the financial markets were showing signs of stress, and credit wasn't as readily available. We were completely stretched by the many deals we had in the pipeline, and we struggled mightily to close even one. The pressure to deliver wins and earnings mounted steadily.

In August of 2008, I attended MDC at GE's corporate training campus in Crotonville, New York, which meant being away from home for three weeks. In hindsight, the timing proved noteworthy. The weeks I spent at MDC were the very weeks leading up to the collapse of Lehman Brothers and the bailout of AIG—the start of what we now know as the Great Recession.

At the same time, GE Capital was struggling with its own financial crisis as the credit markets froze, and GE got squeezed for liquidity. Practically overnight, we went from being desperate to close deals to desperate to get out of them.

When I returned from MDC, the financial crisis was in full swing, and regulators were clamping down on GE Capital, along with the other major financial institutions. This meant that the business I had been instrumental in building was now on the chopping block. Overnight, my job turned into winding down our airport business, exiting any possible deals or funding commitments, and reducing the overhead and headcount wherever possible.

Those months were some of the most formative and harrowing of my career. Creating, building, and growing a business is hard work, but it is simultaneously an incredible rush. Breaking down, decimating, reducing, and liquidating a business involves equally hard work, but it is absolutely no fun.

In the midst of conducting my tasks with mercenary precision, I was asked by my boss to stop by London on my way home from previously scheduled board meetings in Stockholm. It was the week before the Thanksgiving holiday, and London was wet, cold, and grim. I entered our offices in the fancy Mayfair district and made my way to my boss's office, where he made fidgety small talk until we were joined by the London office head of HR. I was not at all alarmed, given the restructuring being done across the business unit. Then, visibly shaken and distraught, my boss explained how even deeper cuts were necessary, and my job was being eliminated.

There are things in life you plan for, and there are things in life you anticipate, but in my wildest imagination, this scenario had never crossed my mind. Less than two months earlier, I had finished MDC. I had been ranked a top performer for each of the seven years I had been with GE Capital. I had been promoted to the executive band. Yet here I was, being laid off.

As the news filtered in, I went numb. I don't remember anything the head of HR shared, although I later found out I was eligible for some pretty generous exit benefits due to my rank and seniority. At that moment in my boss's office, however, I was perplexed. I was crushed.

As I walked out of our offices into the cold and rainy streets of London, my thoughts and emotions oscillated between anger, panic, and fear. A sense of total despair came over me, as well as shame and humiliation. My whole self-image as a successful up-and-coming executive had been reduced to nothing by a mere pen stroke. My ego wasn't just bruised; it was reduced to rubble.

Back in my hotel room, I felt trepidation about calling Cara, not because I feared she would be unsupportive, but because I didn't know how to explain what had just happened. We ended up speaking briefly, and she was obviously shell-shocked when I shared the news. All I could offer her in my stunned state of mind was a tepid promise that things would be okay.

Like anyone else, I had experienced fear- and anxiety-producing events in my life, but this was my baptism by fire to pure, unadulterated panic. Not your garden variety fear, but the kind of unbridled fear that stops you in your tracks. The kind of fear that arrests your every thought, freezes your breath, and penetrates every cell of your body.

Lying in my hotel room that evening, I stared at the ceiling for hours, completely and utterly terrified. I had never experienced anything like it before. I didn't have any way to recognize what had come over me, let alone the tools to deal with it.

When I returned from London, the GECAS second in command personally reached out to offer me a new role back in Stamford, preserving my seniority and compensation. At the same time, the owner of the Austin-based business we acquired invited me to be part of buying out GE. Having these options was nice, and when I ultimately made a decision, the worst of my fear dissipated, but the episode had left its mark, and the wounds were only superficially healed.

Like the invincible warrior Achilles in Greek mythology, my Achilles heel had been exposed, and I was no longer invulnerable. Fear had eaten away at my alpha male confidence and internal fortitude. Unsure how to interpret the anxiety holding me hostage, I had no way of expressing or processing my emotions. I didn't even know how to share my experience with Cara. I felt inadequate and ashamed about being in the grip of my emotions, so I tried to bury them deep inside, hoping that ignoring them would make them vanish.

On the outside, I kept up a brave face. I tried to exude confidence. But inside, I was in anguish. Of course, holding up that facade only allowed my fear to fester, but I wouldn't realize that until many years later. At that point, I merely had a glimpse of the devastating effect fear could have on my psyche, emotional life, and the way it made me show up in life.

This whole period, roughly from September 2008 into spring 2009, really tried our relationship and weighed heavily on Cara personally. She is a risk-averse person who values safety and stability, yet we had a young child, she had recently left her career with GE, and now I had lost my job, putting her in a completely foreign, uncomfortable situation.

In addition, I wasn't my old self anymore. I had changed. The stress and anxiety made me more closed off, less carefree, and definitely less attentive and affectionate than I'd been. Not that I loved Cara any less—quite the opposite, actually. But when your emotions get hijacked by fear and anxiety, you no longer live in the domain of the heart. You're spellbound by your instinctive fight-or-flight response, and all else becomes secondary.

If anyone asked me today for the key to a great relationship, my answer would be communication. Not so much day-to-day communication, which is also important, but real, truthful, heart-to-heart communication when it really matters. For that level of communication to take place, both partners need to feel safe— and both need to be vulnerable.

During the months following my layoff, I sucked at this level of communication. I didn't have the strength to be vulnerable, to open my heart, knowing I would be fully exposed. It wasn't a lack of love or interest in our relationship. I just didn't know how, so I buried these things as deep as I could, kept up a stoic appearance, and pretended I was taking it all in stride.

In addition, another overarching dynamic in our relationship first emerged during this period, a dynamic that took on a life of its own in later years, with neither of us having the insight or tools to effectively deal with it.

In our relationship, I tended to forge ahead, and Cara usually followed along. Not that she was a bump on a log; she simply trusted my decisions because I sold them with zest and exuberance. I often fell short in including her in the decision-making process, and she, maybe, fell short at times in fully expressing her opinions.

These shortcomings reflected our personalities more than anything else, but nevertheless, more effective communication could have helped us neutralize this dynamic, which later became a wedge in the ever-growing gap in our relationship.

GETTING BACK UP

Life has a way of bumping you in the direction you need to go. You may call it God, divine intervention, or the universe, but I believe there's some form of order underneath the circumstances of life.

Although I had talked about leaving GE many times, I never actually would have. The going was simply too good. There's safety in what you know. This is why there are many more would-be entrepreneurs than actual entrepreneurs. This is why people can't kick habits they know are bad for them and why most New Year's resolutions don't make it to February. This is why people stay in relationships, even when the relationship itself no longer serves them. Change is hard, change is painful, and as far as your brain is concerned, change is not safe.

Through my layoff, the universe forced a major change on me. The safe choice at that point would have been to accept the replacement job GE offered to create for me in Stamford, alongside my prestigious executive band status and my full compensation package, which by this time was quite generous.

I was flattered, honored even, but I also had zero interest in moving back to Stamford, and neither did Cara; we both loved living in Austin. Plus, in joining the Austin firm, I was being handed an opportunity to segue into a venture that was only possible because the financial crisis had caused financial juggernauts like GE Capital to run for the hills. Only eighteen months earlier, GE had paid a serious premium to acquire 50 percent of this boutique airport development firm, and in the next twelve months, I would own that 50 percent for a fraction of the cost. Yes, there was a lot of risk on this path. The deal pipeline had been decimated with GE's exit, and we would have to rebuild the business almost from scratch. But I sensed opportunity, so despite my self-doubt and banged-up self-confidence, I somehow found the cojones to venture into the unknown. This pattern has repeated itself many times in my life. I guess I need help finding the fork in the road, but once shown it, I am good to go.

I finally left GECAS in February 2009, since the company asked me to stay on a few months to transition my responsibilities and hand over my board seats. These extra months were welcomed, as they allowed me to chart my new course while still getting paid.

The country was in the depths of the financial crisis, and many people wondered if I had lost my marbles in passing up a cushy corporate gig for an uncertain venture. Maybe I *only* had eyes for the opportunities, and that's what downplayed the risks in my mind. The brain has a funny way of only seeking validation for those things it believes to be true. At this stage of my journey, I had very little grasp on the inner workings of the mind, so I really just followed my intuition.

When the financial markets collapsed in late 2008, the magnitude of the crisis wasn't immediately evident. As 2009 progressed, it became apparent that this wasn't just a bad economic hangover from a few loose-lending practices gone sour. The country was in a crisis of epic proportions, to a scale not seen since the Great Depression in the 1930s.

Against that backdrop, it isn't surprising that we had a hard time rebuilding the business in Austin. As we came into the fall of 2009, I started to have doubts about our ability to turn the corner. As the world-renowned Economist John Maynard Keynes said, "The markets can remain irrational longer than you can remain solvent." The business was running out of funds; we could probably make it into 2010. More importantly, my own cash hoard was dwindling. I had factored in not having income the rest of 2009, but without any prospects, let alone live deals on the horizon, things were starting to look pretty bleak.

Although I hadn't fallen into the tight vice-grip of fear I had before, the pressure and stress started weighing on me as we got into the latter part of 2009. Around the same time, we found out that Cara was pregnant with our second child, due in May 2010. We had both wanted more than one child, and not having too much age difference between Sam and our second child was really important to Cara.

Knowing full well that Cara had some uneasiness about my choice to go the entrepreneurial route, I took on the role of the quintessential husband and provider—a beacon of strength, invulnerability, and confidence—no matter that I wasn't feeling like that at all. I had my fair share of doubts, fears, and concerns, but I set aside those emotions, leaving them unexpressed and festering deep inside.

Because I longed so much for Cara and Sam to be happy and to have whatever they needed, I never voiced my reservations about having another baby while we were on uncertain financial footing. By holding up this stoical facade—"Of course we can have another baby and maintain our lifestyle like before"—I created my own isolation in our relationship.

By now, I had a whole dimension of myself that weighed on me like a ton of bricks, but I could not talk about it with my wife—not because she didn't want me to, but because of what I believed I should be doing as a man, husband, and sole provider. This pattern later repeated itself over and over, providing more evidence that misguided beliefs can be incredibly persistent, and my own beliefs were the cause of so much unnecessary suffering.

Similar to the way many women struggle to live up to the role models portrayed in advertising, books, magazines, and movies, men often struggle to live up to the notion of masculinity in our society. For hundreds of years, society has conditioned men about how they should act and behave. Men are expected to be strong, fearless, and invulnerable, all while being good providers. Wealth and power are the marks of a successful man, so his net worth inevitably becomes his self-worth. Men spend years trying to convince others and themselves that they embody all of the ideals that a man is supposed to embody, and in the process, they often lose sight of who they really are.

I can now see how this theme has colored every aspect of my adult life, but it took a harrowing pain cocktail of fear, anxiety, guilt, remorse, grief, and heartbreak to finally crack open my heart and bring me to that realization. But by 2010, it started to color my relationship with Cara. There were more and more aspects of myself I wasn't sharing as freely. I ever so gradually started shielding her from certain realities, like our dwindling cash hoard and my doubts about the entrepreneurial endeavor. As I shielded her from these things, I also shielded her from myself. I avoided opening up about my own feelings of self-doubt, fear, and worry.

There's a real cost to leaving feelings and emotions unexpressed. They accumulate, deep inside, and show back up as loneliness, emptiness, fear, anxiety, and depression. I was terrified about and, therefore, terrible at sharing my deepest feelings, a situation that worsened in the years to come when the need to open up was at its zenith.

But being vulnerable and exposing my deepest feelings didn't fit my mental image of what a real man does. What's more, it takes incredible self-awareness to operate from a place of total vulnerability, and at that time, I simply didn't have it.

PURE LUCK

It's great to be good—but sometimes better to be lucky.

The first week of December 2009, I received a call from the CFO of the Bogotá International Airport. GE Capital had come in second in a competitive tender for a monster-sized development deal almost fourteen months earlier, but the winning firm—the one from Houston we almost acquired—had failed to close the transaction on several occasions.

"The board is out of patience and just voted to terminate their contract," the CFO said. "Are you interested in stepping into this deal?"

There was a long pause, mainly because I didn't know what to make of any of this. Thoughts raced through my mind: *This just doesn't happen. It's too good to be true. There has to be a catch.*

I took a deep breath and let out a slight sigh. What came next out of my mouth even startled me: "I'm not sure. We're really busy, and it's right before the holidays. Perhaps if you could come to Austin, we could take a closer look at the deal."

Nobody exits a deal of this magnitude on the three-yard line, especially not during a time when the sector had recessed into a deep slump. I was suspicious that the airport was using us as a stalking horse to somehow force the competing firm to close their deal or perhaps gain better terms at the closing table. Inviting the CFO to Austin would force his hand, I figured. If he bothered to come, the airport was definitely serious; if not, we also had a clear answer.

Two days later, the CFO sat in our conference room, updating us on the status of the project, the details of what went wrong, and what they needed to get done.

"The only condition is that we need to close this deal no later than February 4," he said. "Do you think you can raise the funds and mobilize a team by then?"

Aha, there was the catch. The operational part wasn't the problem. We could field a team in less than two weeks if we had to, but the notion of us showing up in Colombia with close to $50 million of equity in less than eight weeks, at the trough of the financial crisis, with the Christmas holidays right before us—sounded more like science fiction than reality.

However, the CFO urged us to come to Colombia the following week to meet with the board. He said he would introduce us to a potential investor: a prestigious local private equity firm that had taken a liking to the project but hadn't been able to come to terms with the competitor firm that got booted.

I flew to Bogotá the next week, and except for returning for a few days to spend Christmas at home with Cara and her family, I spent the next three weeks in Bogotá structuring and negotiating the deal. The "patient" died numerous times on the operating table, only to get resuscitated, and we finally closed this super-sized deal on February 3, 2010.

Our life raft had come in the form of a project that dwarfed any other project our firm had done in its twenty-year history. The timing, magnitude, and way this project came about were inconceivable in so many ways that to this day, I am humbled and amazed by the serendipity of it all. These things simply don't happen. Nobody gets this lucky.

But we did.

After the closing, everything accelerated at a break-neck pace. Besides the language barrier we had to overcome, this project was enormous in scope and complexity. Colombians, we came to find out, are masters at making things complex—very complex. We had to recruit, train, and assemble a development team while immediately taking over the development, leasing, and management of this enormous project.

In addition, we soon discovered that the airport concession of which we were a subconcession was entangled in political hot water due to construction delays and dysfunctional regulatory bodies supposedly overseeing the airport concession. This wild bronco was not only big and strong; it was mean and dirty. It was also our company's saving grace, our lifeline, and we went in with unbridled enthusiasm and confidence that we could straighten out this ship and deliver a world-class project.

Practically overnight, I was in Colombia every Monday through Thursday, spending only one day a week at the home office in Austin. Soon, the workload demanded that I be in Colombia Monday through Friday, and many weeks, I didn't return home until Saturday or had to leave Austin on Sunday night.

Professionally, those early weeks and months were incredibly exciting. We had landed a flagship project that rescued our firm from a likely inglorious and almost certain death. My option to acquire an additional 25 percent of the firm was well in the money from this deal alone, and the adrenaline rush of closing and being the lead developer of this whale of a project was reinvigorating. After having been deflated by the prospect of imminent failure at my first big stab at entrepreneurship only weeks before, my ego was now having a champagne party. I started to make money again, which soon grew to be a lot. It was an incredible rush, and I was riding a high.

Tragically, I didn't maintain any kind of work-life balance. Frankly, it didn't even occur to me. Blinded by my own ambition, fueled by this insatiable drive to show and prove my worth to the world, I had this monomaniacal focus that tuned out all other things. I wholeheartedly believe it's why we ultimately succeeded and exceeded anyone's wildest expectations for this project. I also know now that this worldly success came at a huge sacrifice and cost.

In all honesty, I don't remember much of Cara's second pregnancy. I think it was an easy one, but it's quite possible it wasn't, and she handled it like the silent trooper she is while I continued on, self-absorbed and oblivious. I remember Cara expressing some concern that I wouldn't be there for the delivery. I was there, but since it was a scheduled C-section, that doesn't deserve any real recognition.

As consumed as I was with work, being there for the birth was never in doubt for me. Our beautiful little girl, Lana, was born May 25, 2010. I remember staying home for a week, which was the first time I had been home for that long at one time since early January. While Cara and Lana stayed in the hospital for a few days, I spent a lot of time with Sam. And then when Cara and Lana came home, we had a few beautiful days of being home with nowhere to go and no agenda.

Without realizing I needed it, this time with my family allowed me to recharge my batteries. I loved being home. I loved being there for Cara and our babies, and it tore me apart to have to jump back into the madness of the Colombia project after a week in my little bubble of domestic bliss. I knew full well it would be like jumping back into a raging river. There was no way of easing into it or idling at half-speed.

The following months set the stage for what would happen in the years ahead. The demands and pressures of the project were exceptional, the incessant travel was taxing, and the hours I kept were brutal. But that's still just the outer shell. If I am honest, the project's success—the money and potential wealth creation, as well as being in the limelight—were like heroin to an addict. In this case, the addiction was my insatiable alpha male ego. The more success, money, and accolades we received, the more I got utterly lost in it all. Work consumed me.

Being the full-time caretaker of a baby and toddler in happy-go-lucky Austin, Cara's life was about as diametrically opposed to mine as could be. I was still home every weekend and was involved and helpful then, but during the week, she was essentially living the life of a single mom.

Parenthood came easy to us, but not without cost. Our romance took a back seat to being parents of two little ones, and my now incessant work and travel schedule only exacerbated this situation. We did less and less of the fun stuff in life, didn't have quite as many date nights, and even as we needed more chances to connect, we created fewer. This wasn't at all the intention we had set when we moved to easygoing Austin, but it was where things were. While I dove into the work in Colombia, Cara buried herself in motherhood with the same zest she had for her career while at GE.

Patterns like this have a way of sneaking up on you. You tell yourself it's just temporary, but these initially unnoticeable grooves deepen over time. They certainly did for us, and I was completely blind to it.

On the back of our partnership with the preeminent private equity firm in Colombia, many business opportunities emerged, and we jumped in headfirst. I had no concept of how work gradually dominated my entire life. I would casually dismiss any suggestion from Cara that I slow down a little, travel less, or spend more time with her and the kids. I always used the cop-out that I needed to provide, which was true, of course, but what was really fueling my relentless drive was ego, pure unadulterated ego.

In its essence, ego boils down to a deep-rooted insecurity about being good enough, measuring up, and being worthy. In business, money then becomes the yardstick, and your net worth becomes your self-worth. It was almost tangible. I could feel the success and money I had always so deeply longed for resting at my fingertips. Although it didn't happen overnight, I became blinded by success as time went on. The more success I had, the more elements of ruthlessness, aloofness, arrogance, and egotism slipped into my being at the expense of humility and gratitude.

Success wasn't just something I strove for. I came to expect it as if I was entitled to it. For the casual observer, none of this was evident. I kept my desires covered with a thin layer of polished veneer. Nevertheless, the ego has a way of bringing out the very worst in you, and in my case, success truly amplified it.

FAST LANE

I n 2011, the business in Colombia really picked up speed. We were well ahead of our original revenue projections for the airport project, and since we effectively managed the cost side, profitability was through the roof. Our investors were quite pleased with the results and wanted to work with us on other projects, and soon we had numerous promising ventures in our pipeline with tons of financial upside on the horizon. We built a beautiful new office for our growing team and eagerly embraced all the new opportunities this marquee project at the airport was providing. This was a deal junkie's heaven. I could simply not say no.

The airport noticed our success as well, but not in a positive way. Initially, we didn't connect the dots when the airport team became less cooperative, started delaying permits and approvals, and solicited aviation authority regulators to scrutinize our operations. Soon enough, however, we entered the school of hard knocks of emerging markets business. Tacit and underhanded tactics became more open and direct, and in the ensuing months, the airport team's attitude toward us became downright hostile.

Then, in the summer of 2011, the airport claimed the government was forcing them to restructure our agreement, citing a whole list of ways in which the structure of our subconcession was in violation of their master concession. They also raised our ground rent by 40 percent to cover the government's demand for higher concession fees on the revenues of our project.

We pushed back and pointed to our legally binding contract, which didn't provide for any of this. But the airport didn't back down. In fact, they leaned in. The airport's board decided our profits were too fat, and they wanted some of it. Simple as that.

Heading into this process, I was a naive gringo who thought contracts, rule of law, and moral high ground all meant something. But in countries like Colombia, economic power and political clout trump law. Our adversaries had both: the owners of the airport concession were close chums of President Uribe and his inner circle, and they were unfathomably wealthy. They were also ruthless in their pursuit of profits. There's no way to negotiate with morally bankrupt people, as they see no value in achieving a fair or equitable outcome. Our local private equity partners, which included the two largest pension funds in Colombia, hired the best lawyers money can buy and pulled all the political strings they could, but we were outgunned in every aspect.

We put up a gallant fight, delaying the inevitable for months. The airport availed itself of all possible tactics, including using certain back channels to offer us a sizeable bounty (read: bribes) to terminate our relationship with our investors and partner directly with the airport. It was a surreal experience. I wasn't green in business, and I had seen some nastiness in my days at GE, but this was something out of a bad movie.

Real-life exposure to this level of deceitfulness and unscrupulous behavior has a way of dulling your fundamental belief system because that's the only way to cope. It chips away at your ability to trust in anything. Over time, this and many other experiences yet to come in Colombia would harden me and leave me deeply scarred. Once you see the ugliness and insidious nature of greed, you cannot unsee it.

Ultimately, the airport grew tired of the delays. Heated negotiations turned into direct threats and intimidation tactics until a completely arbitrary deadline was set, forcing us to take it or leave it. We debated with our lawyers and investors for hours on end. We decided that we might win the legal case, but that it could take a decade, and in the meantime, we risked losing everything. We finally conceded to the demands of the airport. Overnight, the value of our project dropped by roughly $15 to $20 million.

On paper, I personally lost around $5 million, maybe more. But it wasn't the paper wealth loss that stung me. The way the deal unfolded left indelible wounds and affected me deeply. Up to this point, I had maintained a certain amount of playfulness about business and life in general. Like a cat with nine lives, I had always landed on my feet. Although I had plenty of not-so-positive experiences, they were benign horseplay compared to the unscrupulousness I had just witnessed firsthand. As a result, life itself lost some of its shine.

While this drama played out, our project at the airport continued to outperform all expectations, which triggered stout performance bonuses. In addition, we continued working on various new ventures, some of which were approaching the finish line and promised major paydays, somewhat dulling the pain of the value we were forced to relinquish back to the airport.

The financial success of our new ventures allowed us to loosen up the purse strings at home, and Cara and I eased back into our old lifestyle, which wasn't necessarily opulent but definitely more than just comfortable. It also allowed us to pull the trigger on some big-ticket items, like an addition to our house we had long wanted.

Given my worsening experiences in Colombia, my time at home in Austin with Cara and the kids became a refuge. Although I never expressed it much, I absolutely dreaded my now almost weekly pilgrimage to Colombia and couldn't wait to return home on Friday. At four, Sam was at a fun age, and Lana was a dream baby, so our weekends were a welcome slice of wholesomeness to contrast what I was experiencing in Colombia during the week.

I didn't share much of the details with Cara—partly because I wanted to enjoy my refuge and not relive my daily business grind and partly because I didn't want to burden her with my business trials and tribulations. Since things were going well financially and her focus was on the kids, Cara didn't press too hard to be more included.

And so, without any specific intention or agenda, we slowly planted the seeds for my work-life to become a standalone entity, completely removed from her world. I censured whatever I did share so as not to worry her, though over time, this just created more distance between us. Not including Cara was a big mistake. Without having any perspective into my life away from home, she came to feel left out, and our connection slowly started eroding.

None of this happened overnight. It snuck up on us over the months and years that followed, making the shift easier to ignore and brush off. We got busy with life, and something had to give. Without fully realizing it, that something became us. Date nights became a little scarcer, and getaway trips for the two of us even more so. We took fewer opportunities to connect and remind ourselves of the magic that started it all, fewer chances to create precious moments that become the memories to keep the fire burning. At the time, I figured it was just a phase of life, which is exactly why the dissipating connection snuck up on us, a silent assassin of love.

Love is a beautiful, dynamic, fluid energy of indescribable force that needs to be fed and kept alive. Like fire, give it fuel, and it will rage on forever, soaring to ever greater heights. Deprive it of energy, and it will inevitably simmer down and lose its vitality until it's reduced to a few smoldering remnants. Our love had been so strong and solid that, for the longest time, our fire appeared alive and vibrant, the flames making it harder to see how the force was ever so slowly eroding.

Of course, I can't ignore how I was showing up during this time. My work ethic and stamina have been mainstays of my ability to survive and thrive ever since I left Holland at age twenty-one. When I have an idea, I move mountains to make it so, essentially becoming a predator going in for the kill—whatever that kill might be. It's simultaneously my Herculean strength and Achillean weakness.

There's no doubt the tantalizing sweet nectar of prospective success and riches were feeding my need to demonstrate my mettle, and fueled by my success, I became an even bigger prisoner of my own ambition. There's nothing inherently wrong with having unbridled ambition and going after big goals, but when your self-worth gets tied up in the mix, you're on a very slippery slope. When your entire world is tied to your achievements, losses become devastating.

During this time, I identified entirely with my successes, and I had no mechanism to deal with any failures. Losses are inevitable, even necessary, as we grow and evolve much more from our failures than our successes. But I was entirely caught up in my achievements and identified with my successes. Taking wins so personally had inflated my ego and turned me into an obnoxious schmuck. Taking losses so personally gave self-doubt, regret, frustration, and anger free rein in every aspect of my life, which came back to haunt me in devastating ways.

As I learned down the road, I lacked insight into the transformative power of failure: the enormous upside if you embrace the growth opportunity and the potentially ruinous downside if you let it dictate who you are as a person. In itself, failure is nothing more than pain or suffering, but add reflection and introspection to this pain, and you have the seed of growth within failure. The willingness to accept and reflect on loss—to embrace failure as an inevitable part of life while not letting it touch your core—requires vulnerability, which is the path to pure strength.

I wasn't there in 2012. I was entirely caught up in my successes, so the state of my business largely determined the state of my being. For now, I was riding a rich business wave, but the tide inevitably shifts, and when it did, I was not emotionally and psychologically prepared to deal with the fallout.

THE UNRAVELING BEGINS

Heading into the summer of 2012, our flagship project was humming on all cylinders; a joint venture was well underway to expand our Latin American business and we had a pipeline stocked with new opportunities, including the acquisition of the second-largest parking operator in Colombia and the launch of a startup data center business.

Despite this epic growth, things were not going smoothly. Business partnerships are tricky. They work great when they're balanced, and everyone feels they're getting paid according to the weight they pull. In our case, that balance was gone, and with the new business in our pipeline, that balance was destined to grow even more uneven over time.

At this point, I was not only responsible for approximately 80 percent of our firm's revenues, but I was also traveling incessantly and working around the clock. We couldn't agree on an alternate way of allocating the profits, so we eventually decided it would make sense for us to go our separate ways, with me buying out the Latin American projects and assets while my Texas partner held on to the ones in North America. We agreed on terms by late summer and set a target closing date of December 31, subject to me finding a way to finance the acquisition within forty-five days. The race to source financing was on.

This buyout involved me going all in. It was going to take every nickel of liquidity I could free up, and I needed to somehow fill a funding gap of roughly $500,000. I scrambled to meet with any bank in Austin that would take my meeting, but I wasn't having much luck financing a Colombian-based development business that was lucrative but had no real hard assets.

With my forty-five days about to run out, the buyout was in jeopardy. I'd like to say I kept my cool and stayed calm, but I was in sweaty-palm territory, and I was losing sleep. Within days of my deadline, I finally got a lucky break when an old-school local bank agreed to lend me $500,000 to close the funding of my buyout. The terms weren't exactly what I had hoped for—the principal reduction alone was $25,000 per month, which would put some serious pressure on my cash flow—but since it was my only option, I was in a lousy position to negotiate. With that kind of principal reduction, I had very little margin for error. Any hiccup in my operations would bite me hard, but it was a risk I had to take. To this date, I am grateful for the leadership team at this bank. They believed in me when they could have passed, like every other bank.

While this played out over the summer months, Cara had an early-term miscarriage. Caught up with my business situation, I casually brushed it off and didn't give her sadness over this loss much credence at all. Never ignore nature. A miscarriage is a devastating loss for a woman who desires to have a child. It's like robbing her of the very essence of her being. In my mind, we had two beautiful, healthy kids, so I was okay if a third wasn't meant to be. I was too preoccupied to see how much the loss affected her or how deeply she longed to have another child. I wasn't there—literally or figuratively—to support her and to nurture her when she really needed me.

Thankfully, within a few months, we found out Cara was pregnant again. However, this pregnancy was very different from the first two, which had been virtually carefree, to my knowledge. The miscarriage had rocked Cara's world, so the excitement and anticipation of having a baby were subdued during those early months—replaced by lots of worry and concern about whether the pregnancy would go full-term.

Whenever I go back in time to pinpoint a pivotal moment, I always come back to this one. Cara and I had a habit of getting to bed and spooning before we fell asleep, and we would always whisper, "I love you" to each other. Perhaps it sounds corny, but it was our little ritual, where we connected for a moment in time, and we had done this every night for as long as I could remember. It was automatic, but there was nothing forced about it. It was tender and loving, and no matter what happened that day or what mood we were in, we always had this special moment of connection. I treasured it.

At some point during those last months of 2012, this changed. One evening, Cara didn't whisper, "I love you," back after I said it.

There were no rules to our ritual. Sometimes she whispered those coveted words first, and sometimes I did. Some evenings, one of us dozed off before replying, and during this time, Cara was pregnant, tired, and caring for two toddlers. But still. That one evening, she didn't reply, and I took notice. She quietly fell asleep without whispering back.

During the next few days, I had the words "I love you" on my lips, but I held back. I was waiting for her to whisper, "I love you," first so I could reply, but the words didn't come. Days turned into weeks. Weeks turned into months. We said, "I love you," on other occasions, but we never again spooned and whispered, "I love you." The ritual I always treasured had died a silent death.

As with so many things that went unexpressed, I never asked Cara about it. I never shared what our little bedtime ritual meant to me. Hearing her say, "I love you," as the last words of the day meant everything to me. It represented connection. It meant we were lovers, partners, and buddies all at the same time. It meant everything was okay. But I never told her how much it meant. I was too proud, too scared to show my vulnerability. I was a fool.

* * *

In the last five months of 2012, business was humming along at a hundred miles an hour. I finalized the agreement to buy out the Latin American assets and operations, pulled together the financing, closed on the acquisition of the second-largest parking operator in Colombia and set up a new parking asset development company, closed the funding, and launched a data-center venture in Colombia, negotiated and inked a new partnership for a mega air-cargo development deal in Panama, and initiated the due diligence on a port deal in Buenaventura, Colombia. At the same time, our flagship project at the Bogotá airport was still in full development mode.

Without a doubt, I was stretched, but there was a lot of business to be had, and because of our previous success, I thought I was indestructible. I thought I was Superman.

Of course, I wasn't—far from it. The mental and physical wear started to show. With so much on my plate, I was having trouble getting restful sleep at night. The private medical sector in Colombia is very accommodating, especially for a gringo who pays cash, so I started to rely on sleeping pills like Ambien. This worked for a while, but soon, even double the normal dose wasn't putting me to sleep, so I searched for something else. In Colombia, it wasn't too difficult to "upgrade" to more heavy-duty sedatives, and I marched headlong into the tall grass of the generic Colombian versions of Restoril, Halcion, Xanax, Valium, and more.

At first, very small doses of these wonder drugs worked miracles, but that's never the long-term trajectory of unsupervised use of highly addictive sedatives. In addition, my almost nightly business dinners with clients and business partners were still laced with the same amount of wine I had before—not excessive, but also not uncommon to consume a bottle over a two-hour dinner. Poor choices can't help but lead to poor results, but the body can absorb vast misuse before it shuts down. It took a while for my abuses to catch up with me.

Outwardly, I was delivering peak performance. My business was on fire, and I looked fine. In fact, I lost quite a bit of weight during this same period—almost forty-five pounds in eight months—though I'm not convinced this was because of the Tim Ferriss *4-Hour Body* diet I was on. (Losing weight is not necessarily the same as gaining health, but that's a different subject.)

In essence, Superman was looking lean and fit, but his internal health was declining rapidly.

I soon started experiencing excruciating stomach ulcers, which required more sedatives to allow me to sleep. In less than twelve months, I developed five different infections, which forced me to take a heavy-duty regiment of antibiotics each time. I started leaning more heavily on the sedatives and thus sank deeper and deeper into the quicksand of prescribed narcotics.

I never mentioned any of this to Cara. I didn't want to open up about the weight of the albatross I was carrying. Strong men don't wince. Real men don't worry and fret, and they definitely don't cry or show any sort of weakness or doubt—at least, this was the notion I held back then. Moreover, I was determined not to burden Cara with my bullshit. I didn't want her to worry. She was pregnant, after all.

My concerns and emotions remained unexpressed because I couldn't find the courage to open up. More than ever, I needed to hear "I love you" as we drifted off to sleep, but I couldn't say that, so the loss of that ritual felt even bigger. I felt alone and isolated, and I became completely closed off, unable to ask Cara for any kind of help or share anything that was happening to me in Colombia.

Thus, I lived a crazy double life. My growing arsenal of prescriptions and legalized sedatives traveled with me in complete secrecy. I suppose no different than any other opiate addict, I became skilled at hiding my portable medicine cabinet, on which I was becoming completely dependent to function and sleep.

The crazy flight schedule to and from Colombia no doubt contributed to my growing dependence. Austin, Texas rocks, and we absolutely loved living there, but it's not exactly convenient to travel from Austin to Bogotá every week. Including the connection in Houston, it involves a full day of travel, with only one flight option during the day and one red-eye alternative.

With my imminent buyout of the Latin American business and all the newly launched or acquired ventures, I explored the idea of moving to Bogotá for a few years. Cara wasn't sold on the concept—neither was I, to be honest—but it was becoming obvious that my travel schedule wasn't a long-term solution either. With our son getting ready to go to kindergarten, our middle one in preschool, and a third kid on the way, our family dynamic was evolving. My limited time at home made the burden of care fall on Cara. Something had to give, and relocating to Bogotá seemed like a logical option to explore.

Cara's pregnancy didn't give us much time to spare, so in January 2013, we booked a four-day trip to Bogotá to visit schools and go house-hunting. Cara's parents watched the kids for a week, and on the back end of visiting Colombia, I booked a hotel for three days in Miami Beach for a well-deserved mini-vacation for Cara and me.

HELL ON EARTH

By now, I was very familiar with Bogotá, having traveled there practically every week for the better part of two years. Still, visiting a city and staying in hotels is quite different than living in a city.

We started our reconnaissance trip to Bogotá in good spirits. We had a full schedule with lots of apartment showings in various areas of the city, nightly dinners with other couples so we could talk about schools and life in Bogotá, and of course, we had lined up a few school tours.

By the end of day one, we were seriously doubting we wanted to make this move, and by day two, it was clear that we didn't. Days three and four only put more nails in the coffin.

The typical "luxury" apartments in Bogotá were nothing special—half the size of our house in Austin and at least twice as expensive. The highest-end apartments looked better but were still only a tad larger and came with astronomical rents. The housing side of Bogotá would be a serious downgrade in quality of life, but what sealed the deal was visiting the private schools. (Trust me, public schools in Bogotá are not an option.) It wasn't that they weren't good schools—academically, they were every bit as good as any private school in the United States—but each of them was like Fort Knox, with armed guards and cars getting checked for bombs upon entering the premises.

Moving our family to this overpopulated, heavily congested, and only marginally safe metropolis would require such a radical lifestyle downgrade that we decided it was better for me to travel.

Completely dismayed with we what found in Bogotá, we flew to Miami, where our little Miami Beach escape suddenly became a house-hunting trip.

Miami is considered the capital of Latin America for good reason. It's only a three-hour flight from Bogotá, for instance, with about seven direct flights to choose from. Neither Cara nor I really knew anything about the area otherwise, but we were quick studies. We lined up some appointments to view houses in neighborhoods identified as having potential, and we walked into nearly every open house along our way.

At one of those open houses, we met a very nice broker who took us under her wing for the next few days—a good investment on her part, as we put a house under contract on the last day of our stay. It was a hopelessly outdated home with great bones in a swanky gated community right on the ocean, and it was in an excellent school district.

We had already pinpointed our target move date to be early August so our son could start kindergarten at the beginning of the school year. This timing also allowed Cara to have the baby with her trusted OB-GYN in Austin in early June.

Since we had planned to rent temporarily in Bogotá, we had also planned to rent out our house in Austin. But we had never factored in buying a house in Miami and taking on a complete house renovation 1,400 miles away, and we hadn't so much as listed our house in Austin. Plus, a few weeks earlier, I had bought out my partner, piling on one more giant undertaking to my already overflowing plate.

Between February and August, I flew from Bogotá to Austin via Miami every two to three weeks to first find a way to finance the house, then to find a general contractor, and then to manage the complete renovation of our new house before mid-August, which gave us just under five months from the closing date in late March. Cara couldn't travel anymore, so I owned all of this 100 percent.

Back home in Austin, we rushed to get our house on the market. We had to close on the house in Miami and bankroll the renovation well before we sold our house in Austin. All while Cara was pregnant, we had two toddlers, and my business was in complete overdrive. It seems obvious now, but this proved to be too much. Thinking I was Superman and indestructible, I had created an explosive cocktail of business, financial, and family pressure that had me walking way too close to the edge of collapsing. Something had to give. The sedatives soon became an integral part of my daily functioning.

In my business, I am the rainmaker, and as I've admitted before, I'm a deal junkie. I love to size up new ventures and opportunities, and there's nothing that gets my blood pumping more than the rush of the chase. I am a decent operator, although admittedly more so because of GE's training than nature. Operations is not my passion, and there are other people who are much better at it than me.

Today, I fully subscribe to the notion of hiring experts—people far smarter and more talented than me in a given area—to cover my weaknesses. (If you're an entrepreneur and want to take one nugget of wisdom from this book, this is it.) Back then, this was not the case. I more often than not selected average people to augment my weaknesses, but as I learned the hard way, that is a penny-wise and pound-foolish strategy.

In our rock star–obsessed modern culture, the prevailing thought is that the brilliant outlier is the determining factor of success (and we all want to be that outlier!), but what really drives success and determines your trajectory is the weakest link. If you don't watch out, the weakest link will not only hold you back, he or she can even sink the ship. True leaders focus on knowing and neutralizing the weakest link. Once you take care of one, there will be another. There is always a weakest link.

I didn't follow this advice at the time. I was all about being the rock star of my business and surrounding myself with people who would follow me along. I made some really poor hiring decisions. I didn't hire people who were smarter and better than me because this show was all about me. Worse yet, some of the people I did hire turned out to be disloyal and untrustworthy.

With my plate overflowing, it was only natural that I let loose of the reins of our flagship project at the airport in Bogotá. We had assembled a team with a well-established operating cadence, the project was performing extraordinarily well, and we were in the last stages of development with all areas preleased, so all seemed to be on cruise control. I had personally groomed the general manager to take over, and he had been running the business under my supervision for the last six months. Thus, I left my cash cow and anchor business, and let it slowly drift to the corner of my radar. Man, would I come to pay dearly for allowing my flank to be exposed like that.

Past March 2013, things just became a blur. I was traveling from Austin to Bogotá every week and back via Miami every other week. Our house renovation in Miami was going at full tilt, and with our house in Austin not yet sold, I scrambled to find ways to fund the now biweekly construction draws, which approached $50,000 per pop.

The Bogotá businesses were generating a healthy cash flow, but with the monthly $25,000 bank loan payment and maintaining my office infrastructure, I was practically living paycheck to paycheck. When a large bonus payout due in March got postponed to April, I really scrambled for liquidity. The pressure kept mounting.

We had to move by August. I couldn't slow down construction. I had to pay the bank. My business was growing and required capital, but my house in Austin wasn't sold yet. I felt like a trapped rat. We finally got our Austin house under contract, and then we had to find a rental property to bridge the gap between late May and early August and put our household goods into storage.

Somehow, we ended up with two different rental properties, so we had to move twice before our final move to Miami.

The first night in our second rental property, Cara was in excruciating pain. It was almost three weeks before her due date, but when the pain escalated into the morning, we decided to go to the hospital just to make sure everything was okay. Our little man Christopher was born two hours later, early in the morning on May 29, healthy but three weeks premature. We didn't have a plan in place for this.

Cara and Christopher came home a few days later, and as soon as Cara's mother was able to fly in, I took off for Bogotá and came back via Miami. Our house renovation was entering the final stages, and it was a race against the clock to get the project finished.

With my first two kids, I stayed home the first two weeks after they were born, partly to help Cara and partly because there's something so special about those first weeks. It's almost like the world stops for a moment as you take it all in. The intimate bond between a mother and her newborn is magical. Plus, a newborn fosters an incredible connection between mother and father. You created this little soul together, and there's so much magic in enjoying that if you allow the world to stop for just a moment or two.

I didn't do this when my little man Christopher was born. I allowed myself to get sucked right back into my tornado of business ventures and obligations. In my defense, I was drowning, and there were real fires to put out, but in hindsight, all those fires were transitory. I failed to pause for one of the greatest moments in life.

I also failed to prioritize my wife and her needs. I took care of Cara and our family in all the ways I knew how, and my family lacked absolutely nothing—except me. I wasn't there. I was showing up everywhere else, but the stresses and pressure were shutting me down emotionally.

As I teetered on this impossible balancing act, on June 22, I learned that Marc, one of my oldest and dearest friends since childhood, had been killed in a motorcycle accident. Marc was like a brother to me. Age-wise, he slotted right between my middle brother and me. He was the fourth of our posse.

Marc's sudden death rocked my world and broke my heart. I was overcome with grief and had zero emotional reserves left to deal with it. In the weeks after his death, an overriding sense of sadness came over me. I felt empty and alone. I spent entire evenings in my apartment in Bogotá, just staring at the ceiling.

At the same time, Cara was nursing an infant, recovering from the premature delivery of Chris, taking care of two toddlers, and preparing to move three states over. For several months, she had been having huge trepidations about moving to Miami. She was leaving her village to start all over in a place where she knew nobody, with a husband who was on the road incessantly. As the moving date neared, the reality of the move settled in. With postpartum hormones on top of the moving stress, Cara was not in a good emotional place.

As these forces started to take over, Cara and I both operated in survival mode, with next to nothing left to give to each other. I wasn't there for her in the way she needed me to be, and she wasn't there for me in the way I needed her to be. Our relationship and connection took a back seat to taking care of our kids, running the business, moving, finalizing the renovation, and all the other mundane things of life that keep you busy. Somewhere in the mix, we lost the sweet little words, the gentle touches, the knowing glances—all the little things that remind the other person that you care, that you see them, that you love and value them.

We never lost our ability to run the household like Swiss clockwork, but all the moving parts were taking an undeniable toll on our relationship.

THE BIG CLEANSE

In many ways, this chapter is the hardest to write. It forces me to relive a part of my life I simply don't associate with anymore, as if I am writing about another person I once knew. I am no longer that person, but it remains brutally confronting to recount these events—and the ones described here are only the tip of the iceberg.

In remembering this period, I am forced to face how I watered down my values and sold my soul, driven by an insatiable ego-driven desire for the shallow gain of money and so-called worldly success. I also recognize that all of it was perfect, in that it got me to where I am today.

We moved to Miami in August of 2013 when Sam was starting kindergarten, Lana was three, and Chris was just three months old. We hired a full-time nanny so Cara would have help, and with the boxes barely unpacked, I was off traveling again.

By this time, my investment partners and I had acquired the second-largest parking operator in Colombia and funded a data-center startup, and now we were in hot pursuit of a very large airport project in Panama and a port project in Buenaventura. I was making oodles of money. The fee flow from these projects was staggering, but so were the headaches of managing these ventures. As the demands of the new projects increased, I spent less and less time on our flagship project at the airport.

Moving to Miami cut down on my commute time, but it didn't lessen the time I spent on the road. Even when I was home, my mind was so preoccupied that I might as well have stayed in Bogotá. I wasn't a completely helpless father, but I was short with the kids and quickly agitated by even the smallest demands for attention.

Looking back, I can't even imagine how lonely Cara must have been during this time. She was living in a new place, where she knew no one, in a city whose culture is far from the friendly Texas style of Austin, with a kindergartener, a toddler, and an infant. When I was home, I never made time to take her on a date or make her feel special or cared for. I just threw money at the problem—at her. I bought her a new car when she mentioned once she might like to have a minivan. When she said she was so tired from doing everything by herself, I told her to have our nanny go full-time. She didn't want my money; she just wanted my love and attention. Money, unfortunately, was the only currency I knew how to give.

Now I understand that I built walls around my heart because I simply couldn't cope with what I had become, but to this day, I feel regret for how lonely Cara must have felt within our marriage.

Outwardly, I was a high-flying business owner, printing money with all the accoutrements that come with worldly success. Inside, I was slowly dying. As I drifted further away from my true self, the only respite was more numbing. More drinking, marijuana, and pills. My ego was burnt on ever more success, bigger projects, more money, and higher status among my peers. It was a death spiral lived in the fast lane and bound to end badly.

* * *

Around October 2013, the first major crack in the armor surfaced. A manager of our flagship project had violated our internal protocols and engaged in some questionable business dealings with acquaintances (read: drinking buddies) and was involved in an even more questionable business dealing with the boyfriend of an employee.

When these incidents came to light, our lawyers investigated, the manager was let go, and then all hell broke loose. He wrote a completely unfounded letter to my private equity partners, and worse, he sent copies to the pension funds that invested in our flagship project. The manager made wild allegations that he was acting on my direction. He also made some hurtful and false accusations that scared innocent bystanders: he suggested that I had paid for my assistant's breast implants, which was devastating to her as well as ironic because she didn't have implants.

Regardless, the damage was done. The letter prompted an investigation by the private equity firm that took almost five months to conclude. During this time, I was allowed to continue to operate the business, but I was under close surveillance, so to speak, and I had to pay for the forensic audit and legal costs of the investigation. They ultimately found no wrongdoing on my part, apart from an accounting error that was outside my responsibility, though I did have to repay the overpayment of certain fees.

Altogether, this whole episode cost me more than $250,000 in legal and auditing fees. Far worse, however, was the effect it had on me. The investigation dragged on for five months, and I was crushed by the immense pressure of possibly losing everything I had built. I was fully engulfed in fight-or-flight mode, now numbing the stress with alcohol, marijuana, and pills.

As is easy to do in all major cities in Latin America, I started to find my escape in late-night visits to strip clubs. Over time, I surrounded myself with other fancy suits who had their own reasons to venture there. But nothing good ever comes from late-night visits to these sorts of places by partially intoxicated, drugged-up guys with too much money in their pockets, and it wasn't too long before I went local—further spiraling to ever lower acts fueled by the need to numb my utter loneliness and to escape the gold-plated prison I had created. You never find solace this way. It only deepens the emotional wounds and isolation.

One morning, I woke up in a hotel room by myself, with no idea where I was, how I got there, or what I had done that night. Once coherent, I immediately looked for my wallet and passport and breathed a huge sigh of relief when I found them. If someone had my passport or driver's license, they could use it for blackmail. How would I explain this? I didn't even know what happened or who might have been with me.

I felt true fear for a few minutes, but then I simply got dressed, went back to my apartment, and took a shower. Before I went to the office, I popped a few pills to settle myself down, and then I brushed off the incident and went about my day.

This miserable existence was my new normal. I was completely shut down emotionally. I was in a dark space, and the demons in me all came out, as the guardians of honor and value left their guard posts. Cara and I drifted further apart, as I simply could not relate to what I believed to be her trivial issues. I wondered how she could complain when she lived in a fancy house in one of the most prestigious ocean-front neighborhoods in Miami with a full-time nanny to boot.

Of course, she wasn't complaining. I only interpreted it that way. She was a rock, a badass mom who was simply begging me to open up and let her in again, to be present and invest in our relationship. But I wasn't capable of going there. I had closed my heart because I just couldn't cope.

During the first half of 2014, we were pursuing a port project in Buenaventura, the largest Colombian port city located on the Pacific Coast. Buenaventura is also a hotbed for the drug trade, and a few months into the predevelopment phase of the project, it became apparent we were intruding on turf we shouldn't. This is where the bad actors started showing their muscle in bone-chilling ways, clearly communicating we needed to stop—or else.

After one particularly threatening incident, I sat in my office, staring at the eight-foot airplane model for what seemed like hours. When I went home to my apartment, I looked over my shoulder. I kept watching for danger as I walked to my armored car, as I pulled into the garage, as I went into the elevator. For weeks, I lived in a traumatized state. I remembered my conversation with Gustavo and understood I was one of those businessmen who had been swept up into the web of some very dangerous men. I had gotten in too deep. Over the next few weeks, I desperately tried to finagle my way out of the project.

Back in Miami, things were no better. I vividly remember Cara wanting to create some "us" time by watching *House of Cards* on Netflix. I just couldn't watch it. The corruption, the greed, the insidious power games—everything that show displayed in the form of entertainment just brought back flashbacks and nightmares of the life I was living in Colombia.

I didn't share any of these things with Cara. I lived in total self-imposed isolation, wrestling day and night with the nightmare my life had become and my utter desperation to get out of the death spiral, to be able to breathe again, to not feel the weight of the world crushing me every second of the day. At the same time, however, I kept chasing more. In all my agony, I still had this deep-rooted burning desire to do more deals, make more money, and gain more power and success.

I believed Cara didn't deserve to be burdened with any of my agony. Plus, I knew she would freak out and force me to do the only sane thing, which is to step away from all of it—the whole business I built in Colombia. But I was in so deep, much deeper than Cara knew. I had borrowed money to buy out my partner, and at this point, my interest tied up in all these projects was worth millions of dollars. At the same time, not sharing any of this fortified my complete isolation, so I continued to numb myself even further.

The grand orchestra of life has a way of giving you the experiences you need while also changing your circumstances when the time has come. By the summer of 2014, the once high-flying private equity firm that had been my partner in all my projects was hobbled and humbled by the overhang of the collapse of Interbolsa in late 2012. This was akin to the collapse of Lehman Brothers in the United States: messy and filled with allegations and criminal investigations of fraud, misuse of funds, self-dealing, and other bad-boy stuff.

At the time of its demise, Interbolsa was the largest broker-dealer of Colombia, accounting for almost 25 percent of the Colombian stock market. The founders had been an early backer of my private equity firm, and that association made the firm toxic to the local pension funds and stunted their efforts to raise a fund with international investors.

When the smoke cleared, evidence showed no wrongdoing on the part of my private equity firm, but the damage had already been done. There was pressure on my private equity partner to sell investments, and our flagship project was a prime candidate. By then, we were fully stabilized and spitting out cash like a Vegas slot machine gone mad.

The early valuation work we did in preparation to market the asset was very promising, and we identified several parties with high interest. On paper, the pension funds were going to get a very rich return, the private equity firm was going to make an absolute fortune, and I was going to clear around $9 to $10 million. With this sale, I would be paid a royal sum and break free of the prison Colombia had become.

We had one potential party spoiler: the airport. Our landlord basically had an option in our lease agreement to buy out our lease at a fixed penalty of $10 million, plus our capital invested. The free market valuation was multiples of that penalty, so their option was "in the money"—in other words, it would be very lucrative for them to exercise the option. We had faint hope they had no interest in taking over our project, but by late September, our hopes were dashed when they got wind of our plans to sell the asset and preempted that move by exercising their option.

The next four months became a master class of Machiavellian deceit and insidious greed that stunned even me and my by-now sorely soured view of the world. The minions of the unscrupulous, politically connected owners of the airport concession pulled every underhanded, disgraceful, inequitable, low-down, and exploitative tactic to wring out our net proceeds. Nothing was spared—even our employees were raked over the coals—and the airport showed zero recollection that five years earlier, we had pulled their ass out of a huge pickle by taking over the project.

As the airport played hardball beyond measure, we all saw a huge potential windfall slip through our fingers, and as this realization set in, relationships on our side tensed. When big money is at stake, it almost always awakens the worst in people and organizations. Greed is a powerful demon. If allowed free rein, it quickly blurs the lines between what's right and what's more favorable.

As the operating partner, I was downstream in the profit waterfall, and my once princely sum threatened to be less than the debt I still had with my banks in the United States. Moreover, as a gringo in Colombia, I had essentially no legal recourse. I was entirely at the behest of my private equity partners. What I would eventually be paid was up to their interpretation of my agreement with them.

As I swam in this murky backwater of lawlessness, greed, and corruption, it became so clear that I needed to get out of Colombia at all costs. I decided this was going to be my last stand, no matter where it landed.

During the last four months of 2014, while we were dealing with the sale and transition to the airport, I negotiated my exit from my other projects with my private equity partners so that I would be completely finished in Colombia after we closed on our flagship project. I left some money on the table, but at this point, I didn't care anymore. I just wanted out.

In a mere three months, I unwound my entire business in Colombia, which had taken five years to build. At one point, we had around fifty-five direct employees and a few hundred subcontractors we used for services. And just as quickly and almost as surreally as the original project had come our way, the end of it was upon us.

The final months were gut-wrenching on so many levels, but the one thing I care to remember is the amazing people who worked for me. Their warmth, loyalty, and humanity touched me deeply, especially in contrast to the many unthinkable actions everyone else thought were fair game.

When the dust finally settled in January 2015, I ended up doing fine—nowhere near the original sum anticipated, but still a significant amount by any standard.

Looking back now, I am grateful for it all. I was rescued from a game of insidious power and greed that had corrupted my soul and from which I couldn't extricate myself. I don't even dare to think of what would have happened to me if I wasn't granted this "fortunate" exit from Colombia. Even when it doesn't feel or look that way in the moment, you are actually never knocked off your path in life, only nudged onto it.

TOTALLY EMPTY

As I boarded the airplane for Miami, the significance of the moment engulfed me. Although I did return a few times to tie up loose ends, this was essentially my final flight back from Bogotá. My emotions took hold of me as the plane pulled back from the gate and taxied to the runway. I knew deep down that I was witnessing, in real-time, the closing of a major chapter of my life, an experience that had shaped me in profound ways. I was elated, and at the same time, a wave of sadness came over me, as if I knew what was to come.

Ever since I became serious about my career, education, and what I then thought of as being successful, I single-mindedly focused on "making it." I bought the American dream hook, line, and sinker. I was a man on a mission, pursuing what I thought was going to make me happy and fulfilled: a beautiful house, millions of dollars, nice cars, luxury vacations, and many other lifestyle perks, and of course, the beautiful wife and gorgeous kids. And by now, I had won the game. I had it all.

So, why do I feel totally empty?

That thought consumed me during the months following my last flight from Bogotá. I had decided to take it easy while I was winding down my business in Colombia. I had made a very nice seven-figure cash-out, and on paper, I was rich by most accounts.

Yet, despite having no real financial worries, despite having tons of time on my hands, despite living in a multi-million-dollar home in one of the most prestigious ocean-front gated communities in Miami, with a beautiful wife and healthy kids and the cars, toys, and all the other things I ever wanted, I felt utterly deflated.

Here I was with all the things I thought I would need to be happy, and I was completely unfulfilled. It felt like I had spent twenty years climbing to the mountain top, only to find out the view actually sucks. I was lost. If all that I had now wasn't giving me happiness, what would? Why wasn't this making me happy? Why did everyone else seem to be happy with these things and not me?

I wanted so badly to be happy with the money, toys, and perfect family. I just couldn't understand the emptiness I was feeling. I wanted so badly to shove it away. I thought the answer was to get busy again, to suit up for more deals, to feed the deal junkie in me, and get my mojo back. Maybe if I made more money and had even more power, I could buy an even bigger house, and that would make me feel whole.

So I reverted to what I knew. I crafted a pitchbook and reached out to my investor network, and soon, I had appointments lined up for weeks on end, and I was back in business.

Except it didn't work. Although not my best work perhaps, my strategy and pitchbook were solid and should have brought in ample business, but I found myself pitching with zero inspiration. My heart simply wasn't in it, and I got absolutely nowhere. Losing my golden touch only amplified my anguish and lack of fulfillment. Now even my biggest talent—my rainmaker skills— were failing me.

It was even more than that, however. Something was missing. Pursuing business like I had for two decades simply wasn't enticing anymore. Although I didn't want to admit it, I knew deep down that I craved meaning, something beyond making more money. I didn't realize this at the time, but my soul, corrupted by greed and the lust for power, was waking up, like a lion from a trance-like sleep, and as I soon found out, this lion wasn't going back to bed.

I somehow managed to pull together a small lifestyle investment deal that involved buying a hospitality asset in the Florida Keys. With a few friends and neighbors as coinvestors and me as the lead investor and managing partner, we acquired a well-known hotel and restaurant operation on prime oceanfront land. Our thought was that we might franchise and expand the concept and flip it for a nice gain in a few years. Although the deal wasn't enormous, this business did come with close to one hundred employees during the peak season, and it was open 365 days a year, so it was a real business by every account.

To make it happen, I signed an unlimited personal guarantee to secure the financing, something I had been able to avoid my whole professional career. This deal came back to haunt me in a big way.

Living full-time at home only exacerbated the sense of loneliness for both Cara and me. We had become two strangers sharing a household and family, but we were holding on to the remnants of a love connection that had deeply eroded. Feeling lonely in a love relationship is perhaps the deepest loneliness you can feel. I can only imagine the heartbreak it was for Cara as I closed myself off to her. As the months went by, I sank deeper into my black hole of sorrow and despair.

From this place of unhappiness, unease, and disillusionment, I embarked on a quest for meaning and spirituality. I longed for answers, although I had no idea where to go or what to look for. I just knew that the old ways of doing things weren't working. I felt I had to be missing something. I didn't know what, so I started searching.

Like the total alpha male I was, I went after the spiritual quest hard and furious. Starting with just a handful of books, the quest eventually encompassed countless podcasts, online courses, conferences, studies of sacred and religious texts, gurus and soothsayers, astrology and tarot sessions, a three-week yoga teacher certification course, and many spiritual and self-development retreats.

My search for meaning was slow and arduous because I was hell-bent on figuring this out by myself. I was too proud to ask for help or even signal I needed help. In my despair, I was as tenacious and relentless as a street dog. I was so desperate to find a way out, to escape the hellish confinement of my own mind.

Ultimately, my search helped me find a path out of the darkness, but for now, the darkness was fucking dark. I understand depression now like only a cancer survivor truly knows what it's like to battle cancer. I understand desperation. I understand what it feels like to see no way out, to feel so isolated, alone, and wrapped in sadness that not being here anymore seems like a really appealing alternative.

If you are there right now, just know that I see you, I feel you, and I can tell you there is light, even though you can't see it. You are loved. Please ask for help because you're not alone.

WHEN EVERYTHING COMES APART

Whenever you think you have hit rock bottom, you have not. That's a promise. Just as you can't really connect the dots in life except through the rearview mirror, you can't really determine rock bottom until you're on the way back up.

I wasn't honest about any aspect of my life to anyone, including myself. My marriage was in shambles, but we were such good actors that the outside world believed the fairy tale we held up for appearances. I made up bullshit stories about my business doing well when I knew it wasn't going anywhere.

Worst of all, I had become an arrogant, inconsiderate, miserable asshole.

The day I realized this truth was the first baby step to waking up. The day I truly *owned* that fact came much later.

I know it's hard to feel pity for someone who appears to have everything, but I believe it's almost worse when you are the person who has it all. You don't have the convenient excuse that a lack of something is the cause of your suffering. You are confronted with the unforgiving reality that you are your own cause of suffering.

Realizing I was an asshole was a rude awakening, but as I looked in the mirror, I simply could not lie to myself any longer. From the outside, I looked like a rock star. I had climbed the social ladder, I was wading in wealth, and I was successful. I was the shit. The truth was that I had watered down my ethics, sullied my core values, dishonored my wedding vows, was barely showing up for my kids—the list goes on. I was appalled, truly disgusted even, at the person I saw in the mirror.

My soul had started to awaken, and I could no longer live in the many inauthentic ways I had been living. I couldn't lie to myself anymore. I somehow knew that to overcome whatever had happened in my life, I first had to overcome myself.

From the point of realization, I started taking small steps, some forward and some false starts. I saw no path to reconciling my marriage, so I pushed for a trial separation, which proved to be as useless as rearranging the deck chairs on the *Titanic*. To protect our kids—and keep the outside story intact—we decided that during the week, under the disguise of traveling for business, I would live in a little rented house and then spend the weekends at home.

This experiment failed for many reasons, mostly because we weren't only lying to the outside world; we were also lying to ourselves. We reorganized our living arrangements, but neither of us did anything to change our relationship, me in the least. I played bachelor during the week and husband on the weekends, continuing to live in complete and utter inauthenticity.

My lesson from this period: if you're going to experiment with a trial separation, organize it like a real separation—what a divorce scenario would look like. Don't pretty it up to make it more palatable or socially convenient. Instead, truly experience what a separation would look and feel like. You might find out that fighting for your loved one is a much better option, or you might confirm what you already suspected and then move toward a divorce from a place of love and mutual respect.

Our trial separation was overshadowed by the loss of my father, who succumbed to Parkinson's disease in the spring of 2017. That summer, in a haphazard effort to reconcile our broken marriage, I moved back home. The haphazardness was entirely mine. I wasn't in a place mentally, emotionally, or spiritually to step up and be the man I needed to be to have a fighting chance at doing my part in saving our marriage. I wasn't yet ready to live in a truly authentic way, to open my heart and share my fears and insecurities and be truly vulnerable with Cara or anyone else.

In general, I don't have regrets in life because I believe everything happens exactly the way it's supposed to, but if there is one piece I would do over, it would be the summer of 2017.

From what I know now, I would have fought like a lion to save and rebuild my marriage. I am not convinced it would have worked, but at least I would have truly fought for it. I own the fact that I didn't. The truth is, I didn't know how to fix my marriage. I didn't dare share my deepest fears and show I was in pain, that I was an emotional wreck, that I was lost.

So I blamed Cara. I could no longer see the amazing things about her. Instead, I fixated on the broken parts to justify that divorce was the only answer. It was still too painful to admit that I was the main culprit in the failure of our relationship, so I conveniently owned nothing. While my heart knew that was bullshit, my mind found a way to justify my actions and inactions, and we slowly inched toward a final separation.

Over that summer, partly to lose myself in work while my marriage fell apart, I jumped into pursuing triple-bottom-line ventures and investments by contracting to acquire a solar business in Orlando. Successfully sourcing and negotiating this deal gave my ego a boost and provided a false sense of affirmation that I was on the way up.

I also attended a week-long spiritual retreat in Mexico that summer, and while still riding the resulting euphoric high, I took a necessary step toward living an authentic life. On Labor Day weekend, right after we tucked in the kids, Cara and I had an awkward sit-down that started with, "Cara, we need to talk..."

She knew what was coming. After the words were spoken, the silence was deafening. Fifteen years of sharing our lives together and thirteen years of marriage flashed before our eyes. The finality of the decision pierced my heart, shattering it into a thousand pieces. You would think I'd express that to her in some way, but I never did.

To avoid the crushing sadness that engulfed me, I focused on practical matters, including a raging tropical storm called Irma that was gaining strength across the Atlantic. Within a week, that storm became a violent lady that made landfall as a Category 4 hurricane in the Florida Keys, completely destroying my restaurant in its path of destruction.

I had never lived through a hurricane, let alone had one wipe out a business I owned, and even worse, a business in which I had an unlimited personal guarantee in excess of $4.5 million. Around the same time, my deposit on the solar business I had under contract became nonrefundable, so I had to close on that acquisition in two weeks' time or forfeit my $500,000 deposit.

In a matter of a few weeks, I went from thinking I had it all figured out—a thriving, lucrative business in the Keys, a promising new venture under contract, a fresh start personally—to facing the complete collapse of everything around me.

In a matter of a few weeks, I went from financial comfort to near ruin.

The supposed cash-cow restaurant became a nightmare mission to save my ass from bankruptcy, the solar business languished because I had no time to invest in it, and the divorce I thought would set my heart free proved to be only the beginning of a painful healing process that would continue for months after the divorce was finalized. From thinking the divorce would be my salvation to finding my heart shattered as I trudged through the realities of moving out, living separated from my kids, and the heartbreak of another failed marriage.

In the fall of 2017, I hit rock bottom. Everything finally came apart, and there was nowhere to hide. It was raw, it was vicious, it was destructive, and it was the best thing that ever happened to me.

Sometimes the best gifts in life come wrapped in sandpaper.

NEEDING HELP

When I was growing up, my mom always said, "Whatever happens, always stay regal."

In the fall of 2017, as my life disintegrated before my eyes, I clung to my mom's wise words as the last thread keeping me from sliding into the proverbial abyss of utter darkness. On top of the failing state of my businesses and dealing with the details of the divorce, I was still feeling grief over the loss of my father. These were dark times, and it took all my strength and willpower to get up and face the day. Many nights, I cried myself to sleep, and sometimes I found it difficult to even breathe. Yet an invisible hand seemingly guided me through that long, dark tunnel. Around Christmastime, there seemed to be some sort of bottoming out, though nothing was completely resolved.

In early December, I had several crucial meetings within a two-day span: one with our divorce lawyer, one with a bankruptcy lawyer, one with my corporate lawyer, and one with Monroe County, Florida. The last one was a do-or-die meeting to find out if the county would issue us a permit to rebuild the restaurant and hotel destroyed by Hurricane Irma. We were coming to the end of our cash reserves, and if the county required us to bulldoze the remaining structure and start from scratch, the bank would likely call our loan, which would inevitably trigger personal bankruptcy for me.

Before I started my drive to Key Largo for the meeting with the county, I stopped at Starbucks for a cup of coffee. Everything seemed to move in slow motion as I headed to this meeting that could dramatically change my life. I was scared and nervous, yet at the same time, a calmness came over me. In hindsight, I understand that this was my first brush with the notion of surrendering to that which you simply cannot control.

In the end, the county gave us the tiniest opening to pursue a permit to rebuild. The hurdles were significant, none of the uncertainty had been alleviated, but I crossed a bridge that morning as I surrendered to whatever the outcome of that meeting would be. It took another seven months to finally secure the permit, and I have no idea how we managed to stay afloat for that time, but we did. In my mind, that meeting was the day I turned a big corner, even though there would be many more corners to turn.

At the same time, Cara and I were finalizing our divorce. She was incredibly strong and determined. After having lived so long with uncertainty about our marriage, she had already done a lot of grieving and was far more ready at this stage to start the new chapter of her life. Even though I thought I was ready earlier in the fall, with the business area of my life becoming a hot mess, I found myself still trying to hang on.

Ironically, the divorce also became a sort of therapy for me, for piecing myself back together and reconnecting with my truth. It was spirituality in action, and I challenged myself daily to show the fuck up, to be a mensch.

In the midst of this divorce, we made one crucial pact: to make the well-being of our kids the first priority in every decision, with our own wants and needs becoming secondary. To this day, that is our North Star, which has made most decisions easy and straightforward. It's not good for the kids if we fight or speak disrespectfully about each other or undermine each other's parenting or refuse to celebrate the holidays together, and we have committed to do what's best for our kids.

Financially, I also had to do what was in the kids' best interest, which included making sure Cara and the kids could stay in the house while I downsized and making sure the alimony and child support were generous enough to allow Cara to continue to be the badass mom she is, unburdened by the financial insecurity many divorced mothers have. This wasn't always easy, especially with my businesses crumbling and me hemorrhaging money left and right, but I somehow held on for dear life to my mother's credo to always stay regal.

Many times, I was scared shitless to commit to paying what I agreed to pay because I had no idea if I could afford it, but I did it anyway. And my commitments have been tested heavily. While digging out of the business rubble, I had to liquidate every pension account and 401(k) savings I had to meet my obligations. It didn't matter. I saw it as an opportunity to show up. I had royally screwed up in being a good husband, but even during my darkest hours, I felt very strongly that it was my duty to at least be a good *ex*-husband. Cara and the kids deserved that.

In fact, while going through our divorce, I committed verbally to Cara that I was going to be a world-class ex-husband, and to this day, that's my mantra, come hell or high water. In the end, spirituality is what you actually do in life, not so much what you think or say.

I have been rewarded with having the most amazing, supportive, and generous ex-wife anyone could wish for. We are really good at this co-parenting thing, and she has moved on to find peace with herself and happiness in a new relationship. I am often reminded of why I married her in the first place—she's a badass, now even more than ever, and as long as I am able to give, she will never lack anything.

With my business showing some signs of life and the divorce finalized, the dust started to settle ever so slightly heading into 2018. As I turned my attention inward, however, it was impossible to deny I was mentally and emotionally in a bad place. I was broken. I had no tools or skills to dig myself out of this deep hole.

I needed help.

I wrestled with those words for weeks. As an alpha male go-getter, the notion of needing help—let alone mental and emotional help—seemed like something for the weak and injured, but not me. However, admitting I needed help was the best thing I ever did. I wasn't going to dig out of this hole by myself. There was simply too much hurt and pain to process. I needed a fresh set of eyes, a trained professional to help me heal my wounds.

Ironically, the only person I knew to call was the marriage counselor Cara and I met with twice before I called it a waste of time. Committing to intensive counseling, three to four times a week for over four months, was the best gift I ever gave myself. It was humbling. It was painful. It was eye-opening. It was transformative.

I had no idea how much emotional garbage I was lugging around until I was willing to truly work on myself. To expose and examine the good, the bad, and the ugly. To look into the mirror without a filter, strip all the bullshit away, and examine the many festering wounds I had accumulated and covered up.

Shedding light on my insecurities, fears, and worries was liberating and the first step on the path of freedom I enjoy today. I am so grateful for the help I sought and received. Without this help, I might not be here at all today, let alone in the way I am able to show up for life now.

Admitting I needed help was a total game-changer.

Getting the help I needed changed the game forever.

PART III

PHOENIX RISING

Lord, burn that which can be burned,
drown that which can be drowned,
and cut that which can be cut...
For I want to know what it is
that cannot be burned,
cannot be drowned,
and cannot be cut...

—YOGI PRAYER

THE JOURNEY WITHIN

In the years following the sale of my business in Colombia and leading up to fall 2017, I started dipping a toe in the shallow end of the pool of personal development and spiritual awakening. With my divorce and business fortunes taking a turn for the worse, I finally had the courage to venture into the deep end of this pool, where the real transformative work takes place.

Yet *courage* isn't the right word, as that would suggest I actually had the bravery to jump in on my own initiative and start seeking answers. In truth, life nudged me to go there. It had been nudging me for quite some time. And finally, when life decided I wasn't getting there fast enough, it nudged me a little harder. Without these painful and dire personal and professional circumstances, I wouldn't have started searching deeper, at least not when I did. Life was happening for me. As I learned, we are never knocked off our path, merely onto it.

Over the next few years, I searched deeper and deeper, embarking on what I've come to call my journey within. My quest for truth became my personal spiritual crusade. I read, studied, attended, participated, and enrolled in just about every book, course, workshop, or retreat I could find, and I consulted with countless healers, spiritual teachers, Buddhist monks, Zen masters, life coaches, astrologists, tarot readers, shamans, medicine women, and just about anyone else that I thought might be able to guide me to the answers I was seeking. It's safe to say I left very few stones unturned.

In essence, the journey within is the spiritual tussle with the invisible opponent, which is you. You are your own blind spot, always. This tussle is tricky, as your small self or ego—and the whole world as you have come to know it—seems very real and doesn't like to be challenged. The journey within is about closely examining and observing the ego to see how it runs your life and how it colors the lens through which you experience life, including your perception of reality and your perception of self.

Now, becoming a critical and impartial observer of everything you have always believed is a daunting task. It involves rethinking your whole construct of life, everything you have always known to be true.

> "Reality is merely an illusion, albeit a very persistent one."
> —ALBERT EINSTEIN

The hardest part of the journey within is that you set sail to a destination unknown. As the shoreline fades on the distant horizon of who you once were, you're utterly alone in a sea of nothingness. Your old life had a familiar framework and construct, which gave the ego the illusion of safety and control, which it is always seeking. When these familiar frameworks and constructs start coming apart, you enter the dark, solitary night of the soul, and the unraveling begins. Only after everything comes apart can you piece it back together in a new and different way. This process is also called spiritual awakening, and it quite literally involves your soul coming alive and rising up to take over the controls from your ego. In this process, the ego becomes the servant to the master, which is the soul.

In Vedic wisdom traditions, spiritual awakening is reflected in the concept of Maya, which literally means "illusion" and points to the fact that our entire world is an illusion—something that seems to be real in our sensory experience and yet is not what it seems. Maya is the veil that prevents us from seeing the real nature of the world around us, and spiritual awakening is the piercing of this veil so that we no longer live in the illusion.

This journey within talk probably sounds like modern, spiritual woo-woo to some of you. I get it; I am an Ivy League–educated businessman, and these concepts were once foreign to me too. At the same time, however, as I studied, I couldn't ignore the fact that what I was reading and learning felt true.

The deeper I delved into these things, the more surprised I was to find that all of this wisdom had always been hiding in plain sight. Mahatma Gandhi, Albert Einstein, Aristotle, Plato, Marcus Aurelius, Jesus, Buddha, Thomas Edison, Andrew Carnegie, John D. Rockefeller, Jiddu Krishnamurti, Henry Ford, Nikola Tesla, Winston Churchill—the greatest leaders, thinkers, authors, teachers, and scientists in history all directed us, in the language of their time, to these universal truths about the nature of reality.

As I immersed myself in everything from behavioral psychology to neuroscience to quantum physics to metaphysics to personal development to mindset work, and as I immersed myself in ancient wisdom teachings, I was able to piece together a completely new perception of reality. I uncovered many things I simply didn't know I didn't know, and in the process, I changed.

I came face-to-face with how lost I was. I had been searching for happiness, joy, and fulfillment in money, success, power, recognition, and material possessions, yet the happiness, joy, and fulfillment I found was always fleeting. It never lasted. Like a short dopamine rush, it would wear off, and I would go search for my next fix.

During my journey, I started asking why these things could not provide lasting satisfaction. Why was it never enough? Over time, I discovered that never enoughitis—the disease of our modern, postwar society and culture of consumerism—can only be eradicated from within. The rest of part 3 describes the lessons that pierced the veil, awakened my soul, and freed me from the curse of never enoughitis.

I am no longer the person I described in the first two parts of this book. In some ways, it's hard to relate to that person anymore because, as I changed, my entire world shifted.

The process of how the human mind learns and expands is fascinating. You've probably already experienced this. Maybe you remember a high school math class where a new concept was introduced, and initially, it made no sense. No matter how hard you tried, the dots didn't connect—until they did. Suddenly, out of nowhere, you get it. For lack of a better analogy, that's what spiritual awakening is like. What you previously could not see, now you cannot unsee. What you now know, you cannot unknow.

As shown in figure 1, there are really only three forms of knowing: (1) the things we know, (2) the things we know we don't know, and (3) the things we don't know we don't know.

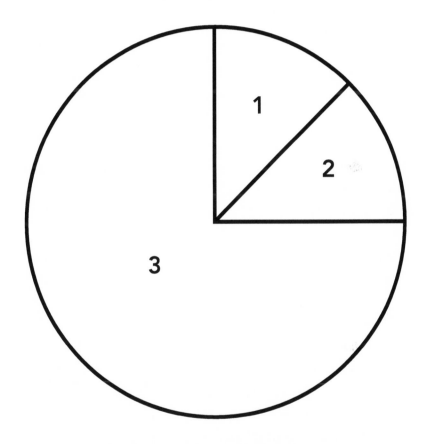

The relative sizes of the areas in figure 1 aren't based on scientific study, but they illustrate the bigger point that we tend to live our lives under the assumption life consists of what we know and what we don't know, but this isn't true. The third area in figure 1, which is far larger than the other two combined, is our blind spot.

Our view of the world is very limited, as our brains simply cannot process the concept that there are an infinite number of things we don't know that we don't know. Our whole lives, we have been learning new things we didn't know existed before. Understanding this concept is the door that opens the path to discovering a whole new world or reality you never even knew existed.

The following chapters are a selection of the many wisdoms and truths I found on my journey within. I invite you to read with curiosity and a receptive mind. Be open to considering things you might not have known you didn't know.

> "Our greatest ability as humans is not to change the world, but to change ourselves."
>
> —MAHATMA GANDHI

I have no interest in being right and don't proclaim to be a guru or great mind. None of what follows is original thought. I merely synthesized known wisdoms, concepts, and principles in my relentless search of the truth.

At the end of each chapter, I offer questions to consider as you make the following concepts your own. That said, you may dismiss these truths if they don't resonate; you should only embrace what rings true for you. My wish is that you will find hope, inspiration, and encouragement in knowing that the true magic of life is in uncovering its mysteries so that the light can come in.

Life is happening for you. There is no such thing as a problem, coincidence, or random luck, and the moment you move into alignment with your true essence, life will reveal all its true beauty to you.

If nothing else, I know this to be true: life has a way of rewarding the brave and courageous who dare to venture into the deep end.

"Until one is committed, there is hesitancy, the chance to draw back, always ineffectiveness. Concerning all acts of initiative and creativity there is one elementary truth, the ignorance of which kills countless ideas and splendid plans.

That the moment one definitely commits oneself, then providence moves too.

All sorts of things occur to help one that would never otherwise have occurred. A whole stream of events issues from the decision, raising in one's favor all manner unforeseen incidents, meetings and material assistance, which no man could have dreamt would have come his way."

—W. H. MURRAY

STARDUST

When I first started dipping my toes in the pool of spiritual awakening, I read many insightful books that opened up a whole new world to me, but four were particularly influential: *A New Earth* and *The Power of Now* by Eckhart Tolle, *The Surrender Experiment* by Michael Singer, and probably most of all, *The Essential* by Marcus Aurelius. Through these books, and through some of the courses and workshops I started attending, I learned that the journey within starts by understanding two important things: that you are merely stardust and that the world you see is not reality.

THE INSIGNIFICANCE PARADOX

As far as we know, our universe has been 13.5 billion years in the making, and it will likely be around for billions more. We live in just one galaxy among the countless others we know are out there.

In comparison to the vastness of time and space in which we live, humans are not just small; we are completely insignificant. We are nothing but a little piece of stardust on a small blue dot hurtling through an infinite galaxy at dizzying speed. In the grand scheme of things, our daily lives, problems, joys, and sorrows are totally irrelevant.

Does the idea that you're insignificant trigger something in you? If you're like most people, you don't like that suggestion one bit. You probably consider yourself quite important, as well as your family, friends, dog, house—you may even extend your generosity to include the importance of strangers and the planet as a whole.

This is an understandable reaction. At first, it's a huge challenge to distance yourself from your perceived importance because *you* are all you know. You have been the only constant in your life for as long as you can remember. Your life—along with your family, friends, career, hobbies, circumstances—feels real and thus significant. But this is just a perception. It isn't reality.

And yet, within this utter insignificance, we are each also significant. We are not here by mistake, there are no accidents in the universe, nothing is random, and so our presence here in this lifetime is with divine purpose, and what we choose to do with our life matters greatly. (More on this later.)

OUR ILLUSIONARY REALITY

Humans are preloaded with basic faulty programming that causes us to think that what we see and believe constitute absolute truth. In actuality, each person has his or her own slice of relative truth (read: reality). What you see, perceive, and believe about your life and this world is *your* relative truth.

Nobody in this world sees and experiences the world exactly the way you do. You're completely unique in that regard and always will be. However, so is every other human.

We are all prewired with the exact same faulty programming, so we all have a unique view of the world, and we all think this view is absolute truth. The result is that we have billions of humans sharing this dance of life, each one believing that what they see and experience is absolute truth and that, by definition, everyone else's perception must be wrong. This is how we end up with disagreements, conflicts, fights, and wars based on politics, religious dogma, economics, and more—not only on a personal level but between tribes and nations. We see the ramifications played out every day through every media outlet streamed into our TVs, computers, and phones. In fact, these very media outlets perpetuate these realities because the data they transmit shapes how we perceive the world.

As part of our view of reality, we all believe certain societal rules and behaviors are real and absolutely true when, in fact, they are not. We each grow up in a "culturescape" of customs and values that a person or collective of people at some point in history decided should be a certain way. The culturescape varies depending on where you were born and raised; for example, what's considered normal behavior in Japan might be perceived as rude elsewhere. That fact alone suggests these rules are arbitrary and made up. Just because people carry out the unspoken rules by consensus doesn't mean the rules are real.

I grew up in the Netherlands, and my mother is quite hung up on what she believes are "proper" table manners. A few years ago, I introduced my mother to my new American girlfriend. After dinner, I asked excitedly, "What did you think? Do you like her?"

My mom answered, "I really like her. She's very nice, but you do need to teach her the proper way to eat."

I was floored. "What do you mean? Did she spill her food or something?"

"No, but she holds her fork in her right hand, and that's just not the right way to do it."

This illustrates the complete nonsense of most cultural beliefs: they are simply beliefs. They are artificially created rules adopted by consensus.

Who says you have to be married to be happy? Who decided I need to wear a suit and tie to work, or brush my hair in a certain way, or go to college to be successful? From birth, we are all programmed with hundreds, if not thousands, of invented rules and beliefs on how we're supposed to act, what we need to look like, what we need to do, how we're supposed to think, what success looks like, and more.

The programming differs depending on geography, nationality, social hierarchy, and so on, but fundamentally we're all programmed with an enormous catalog of *bullshit rules*—aptly termed *brules* by Vishen Lakhiani, the Co-Founder of Mindvalley and author of *The Code of the Extraordinary Mind*.

The moment you cross the bridge and embrace the notion of relative truth, you are on your way to seeing right through the thin veil of culturescape. And as soon as you do, you will see how your life has been shaped and held hostage by your completely untested adherence to brules that have caged you in. Until you see the culturescape for what it really is, you will never think to challenge these constructs. You will not think to break free until you realize you are a prisoner in this matrix of beliefs.

The fact that the culturescape is not real does not suggest that all of its rules and accepted behaviors are inherently bad or wrong. To the contrary, many are fine and give us a framework for functioning and prospering as a society and species. I would never suggest that you go about life cutting a path of pain, anguish, destruction, violence, or heartbreak, but that's because I don't believe anyone in genuine pursuit of living the best version of themselves would intentionally do these things. Breaking away from the culturescape is about liberating yourself from societal programming, cultural dogma, and even religious doctrine or beliefs that don't serve you and finding the freedom of full expression that inevitably leads to happiness, joy, and fulfillment. Happy and fulfilled people spread joy and love; only hurt people hurt people. By unshackling yourself from the culturescape, you transform not only your life but the lives of everyone you touch.

The true wealth in understanding the culturescape isn't real is found when you liberate yourself from mindlessly accepting all of its rules and beliefs. You become free to determine that some of these rules are really brules that no longer serve you. There's enormous freedom and liberation when you decide that you will not allow your world to be limited by some of these beliefs. You reclaim the power to decide what you believe. In making all of these decisions, you are choosing *your* relative truth and start consciously shaping and creating your own world and reality.

Keep in mind; your relative truth might not be shared by everyone, including your family, close friends, or people you otherwise care about. Choosing your relative truth doesn't always put you in the good graces of others. It might alienate people you love. It can isolate you. Many people will not want you to change. They will want you to continue to play small because stepping into your power will threaten and scare them. It will make them feel small and weak if they are not ready to do the same. Sometimes we have to let people go but always do so lovingly. Some people are not meant to be there for every part of your journey. Or your paths might merge again in the future and bring you back together.

Living by someone else's truth, on the other hand, will result in you expressing yourself in an inauthentic way, which will create internal conflict that will eventually express itself in unhappiness, loneliness, sadness, or even depression or illness.

The question then becomes, who do you want to please most? I encourage you to err on the side of self-love and always choose you. If you can figure out and authentically live your truth and leave room for others to do the same, it's the biggest gift you can give this world.

RELATIVE TRUTH IN DAILY LIFE

So how do you actually live out this concept of relative truth in your daily life? Good question. What's been incredibly helpful for me is to say to myself, "That's an interesting point of view." Whenever I feel resistance or the need to defend my view or position, I arrest the thought process and remind myself of this rhetorical statement. It forces me to pause, reflect, and look into my resistance instead of reacting from unconscious habituated programming.

Because of our unconscious habituated programming, when we hear any statement, position, argument, or opinion that doesn't agree with our relative truth—which we often mistake for the absolute truth—we want to immediately defend and rebut to demonstrate the superiority of our point of view. The ego always wants to be right, and it gets easily triggered.

Instead, what if you heard the other person's statement as her relative truth? What if it's simply his point of view? Does that diminish or invalidate your relative truth in any way? In fact, it can't. Your relative truth is your relative truth; nothing anyone else can do or say can change that. Only you can change your relative truth or point of view. Why be triggered by anyone else's? After all, it's just an interesting point of view.

Building in this "interesting point of view" circuit breaker has been huge for me. It's allowed me to pause long enough to not let my ego get automatically sent down the rabbit hole of trying to be right and then react from unconscious habituated programming.

When your primary concern is no longer proving you're right, you start creating room to deeply listen to others. A person cannot learn what they believe they already know. Only from the place of accepting we don't know everything can we learn anything. You might not always agree—in fact, you won't—but your level of understanding will go through the roof, and your perception of the world will expand exponentially. You will also start picking up the nonverbal cues and more subtle forms of communication we can all tune into when we learn to be quieter.

When I first learned about the concept of stardust, it immediately resonated with me. This is probably because I had just sold my business in Colombia, and I was feeling empty and depleted, like nothing really mattered, like my life had no meaning. For the previous five years, I had spent over two hundred days a year away from home, and all I had to show for it was money in the bank. I had missed so much of my children's early years, my marriage had lost its magic, and friendships got sidelined. I had poured my heart and soul into growing my business and developing all these projects that were now doing just fine without me. Like a speck of stardust, I had floated away, and life had carried on without missing a single beat.

As I learned more about relative truth versus absolute truth, I started to see my insignificance in a new light. By letting go of the perceived self-importance of my egoic mind, I created the space to understand that *my* truth isn't *the* truth and that the culturescape I lived in wasn't real either. For years, I had been crushed under the weight of expectations regarding how much money I should be making, how big my business should be, what achievements would make me successful, what sort of life I should be living, and so on. The list was endless. It was an exhausting way to live, as each time I reached a goal, I moved the goalpost. There's always more money to make, a bigger business deal to secure, a bigger house to purchase, a fancier car to buy, and so on. We live in a world with a lot of bling and shiny objects, and we get lost in this circus. I know I did. I had a severe case of never enoughitis. But as I started this journey within, I realized all these expectations were just brules that came from a culturescape that wasn't even real. In embracing this truth, I found enormous freedom, which paved the way to overcome myself and my never enoughitis.

As long as you (your ego, really) believe that you are of the utmost significance, you will remain stuck in thinking your truth is the absolute truth. From that point of view, this world is an unbearable place of rigid, fixed, and unbendable rules.

Accepting your insignificance allows you to cross over the bridge to relative truth, which in turn will open up a world (reality) that's transformative, flexible, and bendable. Understanding that you're a speck of stardust on a small blue dot hurtling through an infinite galaxy at dizzying speed is the gateway to break your life wide open with infinite possibilities.

Ironically, the moment we accept our insignificance immediately illuminates our incredible significance. Each one of us is a unique, one-of-a-kind speck of stardust, and therein lies our significance. This universe was and is being created in intelligent ways by an Infinite Intelligence too expansive for our limited brains to grasp. Nothing in this universe occurs randomly, by accident, or by happenstance. Not even a single speck of stardust.

YOUR TURN

1. What culturescape or societal programming is running your life? What rules and dogma have shaped your beliefs, career, and relationships, as well as what you view as possible for yourself in life?

2. How is this culturescape showing up in your life? What decisions or actions are you not taking because of your beliefs about how the world works? If you believe your dream life is not possible, more likely than not, those beliefs about reality will become a large part of what's holding you back.

3. Are the rules you're living by real, or are they an artificial construct adopted by a consensus of the masses? Religion, in particular, has burdened us with many "virtues" and protocols that we adopt without ever challenging their validity. Start identifying the brules that are governing your life. As you do, start casting aside the ones that are not helping you create your dream life and be the best version of yourself.

YOU

When I sold my business in Colombia, my life changed dramatically. I suddenly wasn't the CEO of a large company. I no longer had fifty-five-plus direct employees and close to five hundred employees across all projects in which I was involved. Now it was just my assistant and me. Instead of wheeling and dealing across the world, I was sitting by myself in my home office with little workload.

This shift left a huge void. I had spent years building this business. Even though I got paid handsomely in the sale, now it was all gone, and along with it, a big piece of who and what I thought I was. It felt like the tide went out, and I was left lying butt naked on the wet sand for all the world to see. It was just me, exposed and vulnerable, without any of the job titles, responsibilities, and prestige that I'd come to rely on.

As this excruciating process stripped away masks and layers of identity, I was forced to examine one crucial question: if all of these external things don't make me who I am, then who or what am I?

This chapter addresses that question. We tend to identify with and define ourselves by our thoughts and the self-identity created by our egoic mind, but that self-identity tends to be the roles we play in the outside world: our job or profession, our roles as a spouse or parent, as a sibling or friend, as an entrepreneur, as a go-getter, as an alpha male, as a conservative or liberal, as a religious person or atheist, and all the other labels or characteristics that we believe make up our persona. In doing so, however, we box ourselves into a self-identity we think is permanent and fixed. We literally become imprisoned by what and who we believe we are.

In truth, we are neither our thoughts nor our self-identity created by the egoic mind. We are actually the consciousness that observes our thoughts and witnesses this self-identity, a consciousness that is made of energy that has the power to transform. Understanding this truth opens infinite possibilities. Because you are energy, you can transform. You are not fixed. You can consciously re-create yourself, moment by moment, by simply changing what you think and believe.

Are you ready to learn more? Let's start by taking a closer look at our thoughts.

THOUGHTS

Every waking moment of every day of every year we're alive, we have an endless barrage of thoughts. According to the National Science Foundation, the average person has approximately twelve to sixty thousand thoughts every single day. You are having thoughts right now as you read this sentence. If your thoughts are about this book, you're engaged, and if they are about something else, you will likely remember very little of the passage you just read. But the thoughts will undoubtedly be there.

Thoughts are triggered by our surroundings or a conversation, or they can appear to randomly rise up from a deep well with an endless supply. These thoughts pass, come, and go from the moment we awake until the moment we doze off into sleep.

Yet you are not your thoughts.

From a scientific perspective, the human brain is composed of about 100 billion nerve cells, or neurons, interconnected by trillions of connections called synapses. On average, each connection transmits about one signal per second. Some specialized connections send up to one thousand signals per second.

Somehow, these electrochemical reactions produce thoughts, an endless stream of thoughts. The overwhelming majority of these thoughts—some experts estimate as much as 99 percent—originate from the subconscious part of the brain, which demonstrates how little thought we consciously produce.

The conscious mind contains all of the thoughts, memories, feelings, and wishes of which we are aware at any given moment. The subconscious mind is an infinite reservoir of feelings, thoughts, urges, and memories that are outside of our conscious awareness. Think of your subconscious mind as a huge memory bank, with virtually unlimited capacity to permanently store everything that happens to you. In addition, your subconscious mind is entirely impartial. It does not think or reason independently; it merely obeys the commands it receives from your conscious mind or runs the habituated programs that stem from your belief system.

The subconscious mind is responsible for the involuntary actions that are part of your autonomic nervous system, for instance, breathing and heartbeats. Habits of thinking and acting are also stored in your subconscious mind, which has memorized all your comfort zones and works diligently to always keep you in them.

The processing power and storage capacity of the subconscious mind is infinitely larger than that of the conscious mind as well. According to Dr. Bruce Lipton, author of *The Biology of Belief* and recognized expert in epigenetics, the subconscious mind is capable of processing twenty million bits of information per second, and these impulses travel at a speed of up to 100,000 miles per hour. Compare this to your conscious mind, which processes only about forty bits of information per second, with impulses traveling at only 100–150 miles per hour.

With so much power and responsibility, the subconscious mind is always on—it sees and hears everything, then records and stores it as data. Your beliefs are then formed from these stories of—or the meaning you give to—what you see, hear, read, and experience in life, and these beliefs, too, are permanently stored in the subconscious mind. In fact, many of your current beliefs stem from your very early childhood, even though in adulthood, you are no longer that young person or in that environment.

The early years of my father's life were lived in relative poverty in war-torn and Nazi-occupied Holland. Based on these early childhood experiences, he developed beliefs that we collectively refer to as a "scarcity mentality." In my father's eyes, no matter how financially successful he was in life, he was always afraid to lose his money, and he always preached about working hard and saving for a rainy day.

I was raised with these edicts, so they became my beliefs. I viewed the world from this scarcity mindset until deep into my forties, when I first became aware of and later consciously rewrote those deep-rooted beliefs.

The subconscious doesn't know how to discern between real and not real, so it takes everything at face value. It is impartial and simply records everything—including what we watch on TV, in movies, and in video games. While viewing "innocent" entertainment, we are spoon-feeding our subconscious drama, deceit, greed, murder, violence, and more. And we wonder why we, as supposedly evolved and compassionate humans, are so desensitized to the hardship, violence, and war we see all around us near and far.

Though you might think the conscious mind is directing the show, all the real heavyweight processing, including both provision and execution of decisions, is done by the subconscious mind. Until you start raising your level of awareness, conscious thought is fairly inconsequential in how you show up in the world, and conscious free will is largely illusory. Most of what you do and how you show up comes from the habituated programming in your subconscious mind that runs on autopilot.

The process of awakening, then, involves raising your level of awareness from the subconscious to the conscious realm of your mind. This includes consciously examining and rewriting the beliefs that are held in your subconscious so that even in unconscious "automatic" mode, the subconscious mind brings forth the best authentic version of yourself.

EGO

If we identify with our thoughts—that is, if we believe all of our thoughts are true, that we are essentially our thoughts—then we give our ego free rein to rule our lives.

The ego is a self-identity our (egoic) mind creates. It's a concept, not a reality. All of our beliefs of what we are—beliefs about our personality, talents, and abilities—create the structure of this egoic sense of self. Some of these talents, abilities, and aspects of our personality are true, but the mental construct of our "self" is completely artificial. If we identify with our thoughts, then we make this egoic sense of self real and true, which will directly influence how our life unfolds.

As we travel through life, we have thoughts about our selves. These thoughts can be empowering (e.g., "I am smart," "I am creative," "I am confident," "I am good at _____," etc.) or disempowering (e.g., "I am not good enough," "I am never lucky," "I don't look good," etc.). Disempowering beliefs, also called "limiting beliefs," create a glass ceiling above which we cannot rise unless we change these beliefs. For example, we will never experience "feeling good enough" as long as we hold on to the limiting belief that we are "not good enough." Within the framework of any belief is the fact that we believe them to be true. As such, these beliefs come to dictate our destiny. As we pick up new beliefs and shed old ones, the ego evolves. The ego is an active and dynamic part of our personalities and the driving force of the emotional drama that plays out in our lives.

Unbeknownst to most people, the ego controls our lives. The actions, reactions, and responses that trigger us are a reflection of the beliefs that make up our ego or self-image. Anger at a loved one, a need to be right, a feeling of insecurity in certain situations, feelings of jealousy that are unexplained, the need to impress someone—these actions and emotions can all be attributed to the sometimes empowering and oftentimes limiting beliefs that comprise the ego. In the beginning, it is easier to see the symptoms resulting from a triggered ego rather than the ego that caused it.

In our unawakened state, we are generally unaware of our beliefs about ourselves, about life, and about the world in general. We don't understand how beliefs form or how they can limit or empower us. Yet these beliefs are like a code that is programmed into our subconscious mind that runs the show. To break free and unleash our full potential, we need to expose and rewrite the codes—that is, limiting beliefs—that aren't serving us. This is the process of awakening and stepping into our full power.

To the unaware or unawakened person, it is difficult to discern the difference between ego and what is really them. Because we are unaware of how beliefs form and how they subconsciously dictate our behavior, we are often left to wonder why we reacted as we did. In effect, the ego often hijacks the analysis and turns it into a self-criticism/blame process. When the ego controls theselfreflection process, you have no chance of seeing the root cause of your emotional dramas, as the ego reaffirms itself and hides in the self-criticism.

The first step in becoming aware is to recognize that the ego is made up of beliefs and that these beliefs aren't necessarily right. The ego constantly compares itself and judges itself and others. It becomes offended, insulted, or triggered. We all have ego, no matter how evolved we believe we are or actually are. The need to flaunt your success, show off, or boast, jealousy, envy—even the highlight reel you post on social media—these are all telltale signs of the ego at work.

Herein lies the most essential thing to know about the ego: it's not fixed. You can become aware of the ego, erase those beliefs that don't serve you, and replace them with beliefs that empower you to be the very best version of yourself.

It took a while for me to identify and start rewriting my limiting beliefs. Like everyone else, I created a sense of self based on beliefs learned from childhood. My never enoughitis originated from never feeling good enough and constantly seeking valida- tion, which expressed itself in unbridled ambition and striving for more—more money, more recognition, more power—which ultimately led me to compromise my values.

The ego does not want to relinquish power, so it takes a lot of deep introspection, critical self-observation, and self-awareness to rewire the programming and beliefs, but it can be done! In my case, it took a while because I was stubborn. It took serious threats, losing myself in my Colombia business, divorce, and two faltering Florida businesses for me to finally address the faulty beliefs that were propping up my ego.

Although this process may be painful, it is also liberating. Over time, I came to realize that all the masks and identities I was wearing came from the upbringing, societal programming, and the culturescape at large, all of which were entirely made-up. Once I realized I was living by society's brules regarding success and chose to stop doing so, I felt a huge weight lift off my shoulders, and that opened up the space for me to start becoming my authentic self instead of acting out the Robert I felt the world expected me to be.

CONSCIOUSNESS

So if we are not our thoughts or the ego that is formed by these thoughts and beliefs, then who or what are we? We are the observer of our endless stream of thoughts. We are consciousness.

Although I had understood this intellectually some years back, this didn't really take root for me at the level of deep knowing until I went into intensive therapy after my divorce. My therapist forced me to delve into why I did the things I did to examine the beliefs that were causing me to live incongruently with who I really was.

This process of observing my thoughts was both eye-opening and painful because it forced me to look at old wounds. My yearning for recognition and validation—which showed up in my relentless drive to be successful, rich, powerful, and even famous—came from a deep wound of never having felt good enough in the eyes of my parents, and my father especially. I wanted to be seen, and I wanted them to be proud of me, so I was always out to prove myself. Later, this need to please my parents expanded to include a need to show teachers, bosses, and everyone else how good I was, how talented I was, how successful I was. It all came from the same place: not feeling good enough and having a father that never once told me to my face that he was proud of me.

My father passed in the spring of 2017. At his funeral service in the Netherlands, old friends and acquaintances of my parents I had known since childhood told me that my father never stopped talking about me after I left for the United States. It broke my heart into ten thousand pieces, and I cried my eyes out that night. All I had ever wanted to hear from my father was that he was proud of me. He told others, but he never told me. I thought I had cleared this issue, but my reaction showed that this wound was clearly still there. I felt it viscerally, and for weeks afterward, I walked around with this intense sadness and pain until I once again managed to stuff it away in some deep dark corner of my consciousness in the faint hope it would just go away. It didn't. My therapist raked that wound wide open to such an extent that I could no longer ignore it. I had to heal this wound, or my life would become a movie on endless repeat, and I simply couldn't stomach living like that anymore.

This consciousness (read: soul) is self-aware, and for that reason, it's often referred to as self-awareness. The origin of this consciousness has been debated by scientists, biologists, psychologists, and religious and spiritual scholars since the dawn of civilization. As far as I'm concerned, it doesn't matter. I can accept the validity of consciousness without fully knowing its origin or true nature, just like I can drive my car without fully knowing how every element of the engine works.

Likewise, I can't scientifically prove that consciousness is linked and interconnected with the vital energy often called life force, but on a soul level, I know it is. This life force—Chi (Qi), Prana, Ki, vital energy, or whatever you call it—is the energy that animates the living body, human and animal alike.

This life force is recognized in all major religious traditions. It is known as *Mana* in Polynesia, *Ruach* in Hebrew, *Baraka* in Islamic countries, and the Light or Holy Spirit in Christian traditions. Whatever your religious beliefs, life force is what connects our individual consciousness to something infinitely greater, grander, and omnipresent; that universal consciousness is also referred to as Infinite Intelligence.

Whether or not you believe in God, it is undeniable that life is not random. There is some form of Infinite Intelligence at work, directing this grand symphony called the universe. As tiny specks of stardust, we don't have the brainpower, individually or collectively, to intellectually grasp the enormity of an Infinite Intelligence (read: God or universal consciousness) that knows all and directs all, but somehow, we are all connected through this invisible energy called life force or consciousness.

To our senses, we live in a material world of physical objects. Scientifically, we can dissect the building blocks of anything in the physical world and identify the chemical elements down to a molecular level. A house, a car, your body—they all appear to be solid and physical in nature.

In reality, however, the whole universe is made of energy vibrating at a certain frequency so as to appear solid. Our bodies, for example, are made up of atoms, tiny particles composed of a nucleus orbited by electrons, which are filled with energy. In addition, there's a lot of empty space between the atoms. In fact, 99.9999999 percent of all matter is empty space. If you think about it then, our bodies are not solid at all; we are mostly empty space.

What holds all those atoms and space together? What energizes and activates our bodies? Life force. Take away the life force, and the process of rotting and decay starts almost instantaneously.

These thoughts about consciousness and life force may seem new or odd, but you already intuitively sense that we are all energy. When you have a feeling about someone—good or bad—you're sensing their energy.

And because you are an energetic being, you can transform—not simply change but transform. Because nothing is fixed, you have access to the infinite possibilities that exist in the present moment, which is all there really is. The past is a construct of our mind, and so is the future. We only live in the present moment. And in this present moment, infinite possibilities exist for the next present moment.[1]

---

1   This field of infinite possibilities was often referred to by such renowned scientists like Albert Einstein, so it's not just a hypothetical concept. It's actually the very essence of the whole scientific body of quantum physics.

YOUR TURN

1. What and who are you? Do you automatically think, *I am a lawyer or a doctor*, or *I am a mom*, or *I am an American*, or *I am a Democrat*, or *I am a gay rights activist*? These are identities. You can have multiple identities, but they are not really you. They are not your essence. So, who are you?

2. Who is observing the thoughts in your head? Who's hearing the voices in your head? Those are the existential questions of life. If you can see that something is observing these thoughts and hearing these voices, then you have to conclude you cannot also *be* those thoughts and voices. Once you realize that you are the observer—the consciousness—then you will also realize that you are not your thoughts.

3. How are your thoughts—which stem from your beliefs—driving your life? Do you really like these thoughts? Are they empowering or disempowering? Are they really true, or are you living some version of the life you think you are supposed to live because of the beliefs (whether empowering or limiting) you have about yourself, life, or the world? Use these insights to start identifying the limiting beliefs that are holding you back from living your ideal or dream life—one that's in alignment with your authentic self.

DECISIONS

Decisions govern our lives. In fact, our entire life experience—the whole movie of our life as we witness it moment by moment—is derived from, and entirely framed by, our decisions. To see this clearly, in this chapter, I'll dissect how our thoughts originate from our beliefs, which, at their core, are decisions we once made about what has happened at various points in life.

Early in my spiritual journey, I went on a learning binge, and I was introduced to the teachings on decisions, which are at the core of ancient traditions such as Buddhism and Stoicism. In late 2016, I started studying the work of Dr. Joe Dispenza, Dr. Wayne Dwyer, and many other luminaries in the self-development space who put these ancient teachings into modern language.

During this time, I also was introduced to two books about decisions that had a profound impact on me, and that came to define my understanding of how decisions dictate our destiny. Those books were *Psycho-Cybernetics* by Maxwell Maltz and *The Power of Decision* by Raymond Charles Barker.

Still, from late 2016 to late 2017, my hunger for answers mainly resulted in an intellectual foundation. I accumulated knowledge, but it stayed in my head because I was approaching spirituality and awakening as if it were another project.

It wasn't until late 2017—in the midst of my divorce and crumbling businesses—that this knowledge started to sink in and saturate every cell of my body, and I moved from thinking about spirituality to truly knowing.

The key moment for me is one I described earlier: when I was driving to the meeting with the county regarding permits for rebuilding the restaurant in Key Largo. I had zero control over the outcome. And this one outcome could potentially wipe out everything I had worked for over the previous twenty-five years. It could strip me of every last penny and force me to start all over.

And then, as I drove, I simply decided to surrender.

I decided that I wasn't going to let this situation cause me any more anguish. I gave in and decided I would let the meeting unfold. I immediately felt a huge release, and a deep sense of peace came over me.

In that moment of surrender, it hit me: I can choose how I experience life by simply making a decision.

In the end, the county did give us a slight opening that required months of jumping through hoops, but the complete disaster scenario didn't materialize. The big win for me was the shift in my awareness. I had internalized what I had long studied about surrendering, and I actually did it by making a decision.

The moment you truly connect with this truth about decisions is a moment of transformation. If you read and grasp any chapter of this book, let it be this one.

BUILDING BLOCKS

How and why do decisions dictate our lives? Understanding this concept requires that we delve into some key aspects of the mind.

It's important to remember that none of these concepts and frameworks are new. They have been known for centuries as central tenets of many ancient wisdom teachings like Taoism and Buddhism. The Bible also has countless references of these concepts—it's safe to say Jesus was very aware and in tune with these fundamental principles of life, Infinite Intelligence (or God, Source, Spirit, however you prefer to label it), and how this universe operates.[2]

BUILDING BLOCK ONE: LANGUAGE

The first essential building block in this foundational concept is that *we think in words*. Our mind receives input through our five senses (sight, smell, sound, taste, and touch), which is processed in language or words. There have been numerous anthropology studies that reference small indigenous tribes in Africa and the Amazon that had no words for certain colors or no words for colors at all. For those indigenous tribes, color literally didn't exist because there was no word for it in their

---

2   As part of my personal journey of discovery, I need to recognize David Bayer, as the way in which he teaches these concepts had a lasting impact on the depth of my understanding and my ability to translate knowing into doing, which is ultimately where the rubber meets the road.

native language. Helen Keller had a similar experience in her early developmental years because she was deaf and blind, and her mind was literally blank because she had no concept of what a word even was. It wasn't until she learned the concept of language and words through hand signals that she started to experience the world. So language and words are at the very core of how your mind functions and, in turn, how you interpret and experience the world.

BUILDING BLOCK TWO: THE MIND

As discussed in the preceding chapter, *our minds are composed of the conscious and subconscious.* The subconscious is the primary processor of information, but it is also subject to the commands of the conscious mind. How does the conscious mind issue these commands? Through language and words—language is the first building block because it is how we process and experience the world around us.

We live in a universe created by and made of Infinite Intelligence, interchangeably called God, Source, Spirit, Creator, Universal Consciousness, and Superconscious Mind. The labels themselves aren't important, and they all refer to an Infinite Intelligence that acts with purpose to express itself in intelligent ways in and through that universe.

The concept that the whole universe, including humans, is an expression and unfolding of intelligence by a singular Infinite Intelligence is a core tenet of all major wisdom traditions. Even Albert Einstein, one of the world's greatest scientists, stated that the universe is a beautifully harmonious expression and unfolding of intelligence by God. In Einstein's perception, God is what's referred to as Spinoza's God, named after the philosopher Baruch Spinoza (1632–1677). Spinoza's God refers to God being a singular, self-subsistent substance or intelligence with both matter and thought being attributes.

Infinite Intelligence always knows what it is doing, and it does its work exceedingly well. It has a mathematical accuracy of law and order. It does not stagnate, regress, or falter. It only creates and evolves in a kinetic forward motion. Because this intelligence is the very fabric of the universe, it is always in order, whether or not our limited minds can grasp or explain it.

Based on this premise that the entire manifest universe was created by and is the continuous operation of Infinite Intelligence, the only logical conclusion is that we and everything else within the universe—as a creation and expression of this Infinite Intelligence—*are* intelligence. We are pure intelligence, always acting as intelligence, which means nothing in this universe happens randomly, by accident, or by a fluke.

If everything is intelligence, including us, then it's logical to conclude that all intelligence is connected. This is the concept of oneness: there is one intelligence, and each of us is its individual expression. Physics has come to the same conclusion that at the most fundamental level, all is one, and everything in this universe is governed by an underlying intelligence—some of which we understand and have been able to capture in our mathematical equations and models, and much we have yet to fully understand, as it's beyond our current level of comprehension of the great many mysteries of the universe.

So, why does this matter? We are connected to this field of Infinite Intelligence through our subconscious mind. And you actually already "know" this to be true through your experience. Remember, the subconscious is the inexhaustible well of all your thoughts and ideas, but neither the subconscious nor conscious can conceive or generate any thought or idea except from prior experience.

However, whether we recognize it or not, we all experience original thoughts and ideas that bubble up from our subconscious mind to the surface, our conscious mind. Because those thoughts and ideas arise unbidden, they have a source outside our finite human mind—the field of Infinite Intelligence. You're tapped into the field of Infinite Intelligence through your subconscious mind.

Remember that the subconscious takes commands from the conscious mind and will execute those commands flawlessly according to the specific instructions it receives. To fulfill the command, the subconscious will avail itself of its entire arsenal of knowledge and experiences and then search, tap into, and connect to the omnipresent field of Infinite Intelligence to obey the conscious mind's command. This is the search engine part of your subconscious mind, your built-in Google that can tap into the field of Infinite Intelligence, where all possibilities and all answers exist in perpetuity.

Whereas your conscious mind directs your life, your subconscious creates your life experience, as we'll explore more shortly. Our main problem is that we don't consciously create. We're not aware of the directing powers of the conscious mind. It requires a state of awareness and mindfulness, and we're illiterate to the workings and creating powers of the subconscious mind.

In life, we cannot control the waves of the ocean, the direction of the current, or the force of the wind. However, we do have the choice between helplessly floating on a raft, letting life take us wherever the prevailing winds will, and skillfully captaining our sailing yacht to navigate the current and wind to arrive at the destination of our choosing. This is conscious creation—the intelligent use of the mind as we were created to do and the embodiment of the very intelligence we're made of. Unintelligent use of the mind (unconscious creation) can only produce an unintelligent result. Unintelligence functioning in human consciousness produces wrong decisions. As a result of these wrong decisions, which are typically unconsciously made, we limit ourselves to a life of suffering, which will express itself in such manifestations such as illness, hardships, financial strain, family quarrels, and on a larger scale, wars, famine, injustices, and inequality. It can be no other way because the universe always operates intelligently and in perfect law and order, so wrong decisions yield undesired results, and right decisions yield desired results.

BUILDING BLOCK THREE: THE WORLD

The third essential building block is that *the world, including yours, is made up of and created by language or words*. This premise is deeply rooted in ancient wisdom traditions. Throughout the first chapter of Genesis, God is set on bringing forth creation. He desires it, he speaks it, and it is. God said, "Let there be light," and there was light. The sky, land, seas, vegetation, and living creatures were all created by the spoken word of God:

> Then God said, "Let us make man in our image...so God created man..." (Genesis 1:26-27)

Likewise, you create your world—the way you see and experience life—using language and words. Our minds are meaning-making machines. Every time something happens, we interpret the event or experience and assign meaning to it. As such, your entire life is a narrative that your brain threads together from past experiences, beliefs, and the repetitive meaning you give to circumstances and events. It has nothing to do with what actually happens. Your life is a story you create with language.

THE POWER OF BELIEFS

We all know both intuitively and from experience that two people can experience the same event and have a very different understanding of or reaction to it. What can deflate and disillusion one person can be the fuel and inspiration for another to come back stronger and better. The same event, but people can experience it differently based on their beliefs about themselves and the world at large.

Throughout my early career, I took lost business deals really hard. I felt deflated for weeks sometimes and continuously mulled over why I failed to win and what I could have done differently. My response was rooted in a belief system in which my entire self-worth was based on my business success. Any lost business deal was a mini assassination of my self-worth, so I took the losses very personally.

Today, I no longer have this belief system. A lost business deal is, at best, a mild disappointment, but it does nothing to my self-worth, so I bounce back right away. I can see now that what happens needs to be that way, or it wouldn't have happened. I no longer construct a narrative around the situation that might put me in a state of suffering for weeks and affect my confidence to go after the next deal.

All of our stories are stored in our subconscious mind, and over time, these stories build up and often reinforce our beliefs about ourselves and life. We develop most of our deep-rooted beliefs when we are young, before the age of seven,[3] but we can develop and create beliefs throughout our lifetime.

The incidents that lead to these lifelong beliefs can seem minor. Perhaps as a child, your parents repeatedly said you were sloppy because you tended to leave a trail of toys behind you. Your malleable young subconscious mind registered each time you were reminded of this, so you formed a belief that you're sloppy. Then, as you grew into an adult with this belief, this pattern repeated itself endlessly—both in people commenting on your sloppiness and in you acting out sloppiness in keeping with your belief—and you even started referring to yourself as sloppy. But are you really sloppy? You wouldn't be if you consciously decided you weren't, but your belief system, which operates on autopilot, has adopted this programming, and so you mindlessly act out sloppiness in life. This pattern applies to virtually all the habits and characteristics we believe we have: "I am not good enough," "I am never lucky," "I always mess things up," and so on. The fact is, you're not a fixed entity. Your beliefs are just decisions you once made about something or yourself, but you can consciously make a different decision and change this programming that essentially runs your life.

---

3   Bruce Lipton, *The Biology of Belief: Unleashing the Power of Consciousness, Mind & Miracles*, 10th ed. (Carlsbad, CA: Hay House, 2016).

Beliefs are empowering or limiting; there's no neutral belief. Because beliefs stem from stories made up of language and words, beliefs themselves are also language and words. Our beliefs are the seeds we plant in the most fertile of soils: the subconscious mind. Empowering beliefs, or intelligent thinking, will yield intelligent results—life experiences you want. Limiting beliefs, on the other hand, constitute unintelligent thinking and will yield unintelligent results—life experiences you don't want. This isn't magic, luck, or some woo-woo law-of-attraction gimmick. This is about conscious creation and congruent actions stemming from an understanding of how the basic human being operating system works.

Our problem is that we're not aware of our limiting beliefs, so we can't arrest the unintelligent thinking when it arises, and so we only really "see" the unintelligent results: the life experiences we don't want. The truth is that these undesired life experiences are the effect of the cause, which is our limiting beliefs.

Figure 2 demonstrates how the psycho-cybernetic loop that makes up this operating system of the egoic mind works.

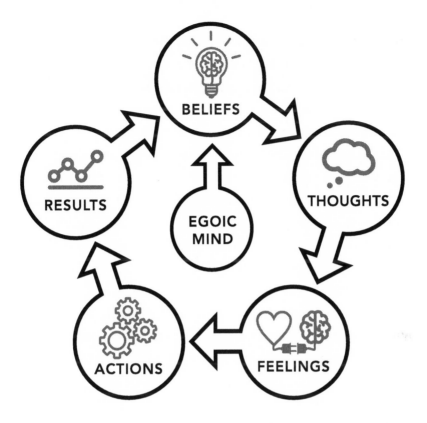

Beliefs, which are captured in language and words, produce your predominant thoughts, which, in turn, through a neurochemical reaction, create your feelings, which cause your emotional state. Your emotional state, in turn, dictates the action(s) that you will or will not take, and your actions produce the results—your reality, your life. The results reinforce your beliefs, which closes the circle of this infinite self-reinforcing loop.

Understanding this interconnected operating system is helpful in cultivating awareness, as you can back-solve quite easily from either the place of results, actions, feelings, or thoughts. There are more intricate back-solving techniques and frameworks that are beyond the scope of this book but are part of my coaching practice and that of many other transformation coaches, but here's a brief summary of the process.

Let's say the same results are repeatedly showing up in a certain area of your life, but it's not immediately obvious what limiting belief might be causing this. Back-solving would involve working backward to find the root limiting belief. You would start by looking at what actions you're taking or failing to take that are causing this undesired result. Then look at what emotional state or feeling is driving these actions or inactions. Knowing your emotional state always comes from your thoughts; examine what thoughts are causing this emotional state or feeling. And once you have identified the thoughts that are at the root of your emotional state, inquire within to determine which limiting beliefs are the source of these thoughts.

Here's an example that happened after my negative business experiences in Colombia, back-solving from the result to the limiting belief:

- *Result:* I was starting to lose business deals or deals would go sideways or just fail to materialize, which only served to reinforce the belief I had formed that the whole world was working against me.
- *Actions (or inactions):* I didn't take action on deals when I should have.
- *Emotions:* I was fearful, worried, and anxious.
- *Thoughts:* I was expecting the worst in every situation.
- *Limiting belief:* Everyone is out to screw me.

However, awareness only gets you so far. It definitely can help you understand the root cause and triggers, but it doesn't really change anything. And since the root cause can only be addressed at the level of beliefs, there's another fundamental and impregnable obstacle, which is that inherent within the definition of the word *belief* is an acceptance that the statement is true.

Beliefs are very resilient, more often than not buried deep down in the far corners of the subconscious mind, and leave very little leeway to be changed consciously. Everything in your life—your entire reality you call your life—can be traced back to your beliefs. All the undesirable patterns and experiences of your life, for example, can be traced back to your limiting beliefs. In this sense, suffering is the direct result of your thinking. Suffering, which is distinct to humans, doesn't exist in the physical world. It comes into existence through the mental and emotional processes the mind uses to create your story. The story colors your experience, which is how you see the world.

> "Suffering does not exist in the natural world, man is the architect of his own suffering by the design of his own thinking."
> —DAVID BAYER

BELIEFS ARE DECISIONS

So, are we stuck with being slaves to our beliefs? No, the good news is we're not.

Beliefs are decisions we made at some point in our life about how life works and operates for us. Most of this baggage was donated to you by your parents during your early developmental years and your upbringing. From the age of around three, your brain is sufficiently developed so that you start interpreting life and assigning meaning to things. Most of your beliefs during these early developmental years are copied from the prevailing beliefs your parents have about life. In that sense, they pass on both their empowering beliefs and their limiting beliefs, as in those early years, your subconscious mind is like a sponge, absorbing everything you see and hear. These beliefs anchor themselves deep in your subconscious and become the lens through which you see and experience the world. Every time anything happens, you assign meaning and *decide* on a belief. Limiting beliefs such as "I am not good enough," "People can't be trusted," "Money is hard to make," "I am ugly," "I am not smart," and so on are decisions you once made that ultimately shaped and formed your beliefs about life and the world.

Understanding that beliefs are, in fact, decisions opens up an entirely new paradigm to shift the thought pattern. Remember, beliefs produce thoughts, which in turn, trigger your feelings that drive your actions that produce your results.

The moment you really see that beliefs are, in fact, decisions, you have given yourself access to true personal transformation. The moment you realize that you have *decided* "I am not good enough" or "People can't be trusted" is the moment you realize that you can also decide something different.

This is a fundamental distinction between decisions and beliefs: all beliefs are decisions, but not all decisions are beliefs. You can identify a (limiting) belief, but that doesn't mean you can change it in that moment. To you, beliefs are true statements; you can tell yourself you now have a different belief, but that doesn't make it so.

Decisions are an entirely different animal. Within the construct of language and cognitive processing, you can, in fact, make another decision at any moment, and that decision would be true because you just made it. The language of decision allows you to make a different decision about any limiting belief that has been holding you back in life.

> "The principle of life is that life responds by corresponding; your life becomes the thing you have decided it will be."
>
> —RAYMOND CHARLES BARKER

The true power of decision is that it's definitive and finite. By definition, a decision rules out all other options. This makes for a powerful instruction to the subconscious mind that leaves no wiggle room, fogginess, or softness of intent. Layering a new belief over an old limiting belief is a weak instruction more akin to a hope than a resolution. When you *believe* you can do something, you leave room for the fact you can't. When you *decide* you can do something, there's no gray area. It's been decided. And in the likeness of Infinite Intelligence, of which we are all just an individual expression, that which we *decide* through language and word becomes our reality.

Throughout the ages, countless sages and wise men—such as Marcus Aurelius ("Our life is what our thoughts make it"), Buddha ("We are shaped by our thoughts, we become what we think"), and Gandhi ("A man is but the product of this thoughts, what he thinks, he becomes")—have referenced this universal truth about decisions. Even contemporaries like Albert Einstein ("We can't solve our problems with the same level of thinking that we used to create them") and Henry Ford ("Whether you think you can, or you think you can't, you're right") have taught us that we create our world with our minds through thought, which is language and words.

Change the language and words of your beliefs—through and by decision—and your mind will respond by producing different thoughts, which trigger different feelings, which drive different actions, which produce different results. This is an infallible process of the infinitely intelligent universe that operates, however impartially, by perfect law and order.

If you are to invest in any personal development seeking radical transformation and self-mastery, start here. There's no such thing as personal mastery without becoming a master of your mindset.

YOUR TURN

1. When confronted with negative emotions and feelings, inquire within to see if you can separate what actually happened and the story or narrative you have created.

2. Your story or narrative—how you are experiencing the situation—is the meaning you give to what happened, which is always impartial and fact-based. For example, if you lose your job, that is what happened, nothing more and nothing less. The story you might create is "I am not a good employee," "My career is over," "I am never going to find such a good job again," "I am always unlucky," and so on. Likewise, you might create a positive story: "I always land on my feet," "I always get lucky," "I always find a better job." The story or narrative creates the experience, which creates the negative (or positive) emotions and feelings.

3. When you have identified the meaning you've given the experience, make another empowering decision that changes the narrative. For example, tell yourself, "I am a good employee; the company just needed to cut costs," "Now I am able to find an even better job with a company that values me," "There are a lot of jobs out there; this is not a problem," and so on. You can decide how you experience an event. Since we live in an impartial universe that operates in intelligent ways by perfect law and order, our subconscious mind will always seek out a match that's congruent with our core beliefs, and the universe will manifest this into your reality. Whether these beliefs are empowering or limiting, they will come into your life. This is how we are each powerful creators of our own life experience, since through our deeply held beliefs, we dictate our destiny.

POLARITY

During my months of intensive therapy, one of the most profound revelations was that I had been living within rigidly defined boxes. I left no breathing room for life to show up any differently than my expectations. Deviations were met with harsh judgment rather than trying to flow with them.

One of my rigid boxes was what it meant to be successful. I had a narrow concept of what success looked like, and I could not accept anything outside of that. During therapy, I recognized that this pattern extended back to my teens, and over the years, it had become more rigid and confined, to the extent that I was now being stifled. It was like I had created my own prison—a golden one but a prison nonetheless.

In early 2014, we had valued the business in Colombia, and on paper, my stake was close to $10 million. By the time we sold the business in late 2014—after legal wrangling, currency devaluation, strong-arming tactics by our counterparty—I walked away with about a quarter of that amount, a huge payday that doesn't even factor in the millions I made during the years I had this project under my management.

Yet because I had defined success as making $10 million, I came away bitter and disillusioned. I felt cheated by my partners, my counterparties, by life itself. What should have been a cause for celebration became a huge disappointment. Had I understood the concept of polarity back then, I would have responded differently.

In essence, polarity involves seeing both sides of the coin at all times, the positives and negatives. Back then, I saw the world as black and white, so I could only see one side, in this case, the negative of being forced to leave money on the table.

The truth is, God saved my life from the toxic environment of Colombia and gave me a nice chunk of change for my efforts. Things could have gotten much worse in terms of payout too; the devaluation of the peso alone could have wiped out another 50 percent, but I got out just in time.

Being able to see both sides of the coin at the same time allows you to see all the shades of gray between black and white. It brings nuance into your thinking. Grasping the concept of polarity can help you to adapt to the natural ebb and flow of life rather than fight it.

YIN AND YANG

The concept of polarity was well known in ancient Indian (Vedic), Mayan, and Egyptian civilizations and is best recognized today in the yin-yang symbol known as the Taijitu, which is derived from Taoism. In ancient Chinese philosophy, yin and yang is the concept of dualism, which describes how seemingly opposite or contrary forces may actually be complementary, interconnected, and interdependent and how they may give rise to each other as they interrelate.

The word *yin* means "shady side" and is represented in the Taijitu as the black half with the white dot. The yin qualities are female energy: softness, being passive, heaviness, coolness, feeling, and surrender. The word *yang* means "sunny side" and is represented by the white half with the black dot. The yang qualities are male energy: hardness, being assertive, buoyancy, heat, thinking, and attack.

Yin and yang are two halves that, together, bring wholeness. Yin and yang are also the starting points for change. When something is whole, by definition, it's unchanging and complete. When you split something into two halves, the equilibrium of wholeness is upset. The yin and yang halves chase after each other as they seek a new balance with the other.

Moreover, the concept of dualism and dependency is graphically illustrated by the white (yang) dot within the black (yin) half and vice versa. Neither half can exist without its counterpart. This is not just symbolism; this pattern repeats itself everywhere around us in astounding ways.

> "When people see things as beautiful, ugliness is created. When people see things as good, evil is created.
>
> Being and non-being produce each other.
> Difficult and easy complement each other.
> Long and short define each other.
> High and low oppose each other.
> Fore and aft follow each other."
>
> —FROM THE ANCIENT WISDOM TEXTS OF THE *TAO TE CHING*

Neither yin nor yang is absolute, and neither one is polarity in itself. Nothing in the natural world is completely yin or completely yang. Each aspect contains the beginning point for the other, just as day becomes night and then night becomes day. Yin and yang are interdependent so that one requires the other to be complete.

Likewise, yin and yang—individually and as part of the balance in polarity—are not static. They flow and change with time. Again, think about day gradually flowing into night. Day and night themselves are not static entities. As the earth ages, its spin slows, causing the length of day and night to almost imperceptibly get longer. In this case, the change in the relationship between yin and yang is gradual; in other cases, the shift can be dramatic, with one aspect abruptly transforming into the other.

Yin and yang and the Taijitu ultimately symbolize the polarity—the continual shift between chaos and order, feminine and masculine, day and night, high and low, hot and cold, sweet and sour, right and left, up and down—present in our lives and throughout the world.

LESSONS FROM POLARITY

Our minds are meaning-making machines. We interpret everything we see and experience, and we assign meaning, typically based on similar past experiences. The meaning we assign might be based on erroneous assumptions, but that doesn't matter to the mind. Remember, the subconscious has an impulsive need to judge and label; nothing can be left uncategorized.[4]

---

4 The epitome of enlightenment or spirituality is having no opinion. You just see things for what they are and assign no meaning, label, or judgment whatsoever.

Typically, these labels are extremes—positive or negative—without room for nuance. When something happens, we label it "good" or "bad," and based on the label, our brain triggers autonomous, prewired emotional responses that are associated with good or bad. But according to the concept of polarity, nothing is ever solely good or bad because it needs both sides to be whole or balanced. That one hundred dollars you found on the street is good for you and bad for whoever lost it. When a lover leaves you and breaks your heart, that's a bad thing; however, if you meet the man or woman of your dreams three months later, was the lover's departure truly bad?

Feminine and masculine are perhaps the quintessential poles or opposites, but in an ill-fated attempt to equalize the genders, we have, in fact, neutralized them. The result is an identity crisis of epic proportions on both sides.

In terms of the feminine and masculine, when equal becomes sameness, you douse the naturally smoldering fire of passion between the two sexes with ice-cold water. You kill the energetic tension between the opposite poles that is the essential, sacred, sensual dance between the two sexes.

The masculine energy is the warrior and protector, action-oriented, single-minded, structured, conscious, rational, and linear. The masculine energy operates from the mind, oscillating between all timelines—past, present, and future. The feminine energy, on the other hand, is the divine goddess and mother, life-giving, creative, wild, passionate, and nonlinear. The feminine energy operates from the heart and lives in the present moment, the here and now.

For most of my adult life, I was the quintessential alpha male who oozed all of these masculine traits from every pore. I chased everything with a vengeance, including my education, career, and women. I operated completely from the mind and reduced everything to rational or logical thought, no matter what my heart was feeling or telling me. It's not that I didn't feel anything. In fact, I felt a lot but suppressed these feelings and left them unexpressed while numbing them with displacement activities as necessary.

When I got divorced, my heart broke into ten thousand pieces, and therapy exposed all my bottled-up pain, unexpressed emotions, and deep wounds that were the cause of how I had shown up in life until that point. Through therapy, I was able to open my heart, embrace vulnerability as a strength rather than the weakness I had always thought it was, and start integrating my feminine energy into my being. I started to learn how to avail myself of my intuition, my passion, my creativity, and my nonlinear thinking. I didn't just become a more whole and balanced person. I became infinitely more insightful and powerful in business, and my newfound ability to express my emotions and feelings helped me deepen my relationships and ultimately become a better love partner as well.

Today, I lean heavily on the feminine energy qualities I have cultivated. They're invaluable to me, and I couldn't do what I do today without having done the work to open up my mind-heart connection. Anyone who meets me these days will still recognize that alpha male in me, but this alpha male aspect of my persona is balanced out now and no longer carves a ruinous path in his relentless pursuit of worldly achievement.

The masculine and feminine poles have nothing to do with being gay or straight. In any relationship, you need polarity to have sexual passion, as sexual attraction is based on sexual polarity. All-natural forces flow between two poles.

This discussion of masculine and feminine has nothing to do with the rights of men and women either. The sexes are equal, and any argument to the contrary is totally outdated. I am talking about the feminine and masculine energies and qualities.

We have also completely missed the target by vilifying the masculine in defense of the feminine. The fact is they complete each other, always have, and always will. One cannot exist without the other. The feminine has always been just as vitally important and critically essential as the masculine, but they are opposites, and therein lies the beauty we should celebrate, not vilify.

Understanding polarity—including the masculine and feminine— opens up the ability to seek the other pole as a way to see the whole. This awareness, in combination with raising your overall self-awareness, can help you shift from being tormented by life to reframing events and situations in a way that serves you the best. Understanding polarity is knowing, at a very deep level, that life oscillates between chaos and order, that in the greatest depth of chaos, the seed of order has been planted already. It's knowing that the good times will not last forever, and neither will the bad because everything is whole—night will become day, winter will become summer, and a bad day will be followed by a good one.

The next time you find yourself experiencing a negative emotion, try to find the other pole. For example, if you recently lost your job, that is a legitimate excuse to feel down and out. Life is handing you lemons, your spouse is on your case about it, and you have financial concerns, so you're feeling depressed and rightfully so.

When you're clearly on one end of the pole—in this case, the negative one—think about what is at the opposite end. In this case, opposite would be a vibrant, happy, and confident person who's ready to tackle any problem. That's the kind of candidate that's going to interview well and likely get hired to a new position.

As hard as it might seem to "move" yourself to the other side of the pole, you can do so quite readily by simply imagining all the emotions and feelings you would have if you were on that other side. At first, this is going to feel fake and fabricated, but if you consistently work on this, you will see yourself shifting to the other pole.

Before you can make this shift, however, you first have to understand where you are and what is on the other side. Whenever you find yourself in a trying situation, ask yourself, what's the opposite side of this? How can I apply the concept of polarity to this? I promise you, with time and practice, you will get really good at this. And remember, even if you can't quite get to the complete other pole, so to speak, just getting back to the proverbial "middle" is often enough to shift the tide. Maybe you don't go from unmeasurable darkness to deliriously happy, but just moving away from the dark and refinding the balance of the whole is already a monumental step toward alleviating needless suffering.

YOUR TURN

1. Where do you hold rigid views or expectations? Where are you thinking in black-and-white terms?

2. How is this rigid thinking affecting your life? Chances are that if you label things as strictly good or bad, you are experiencing anger, sadness, irritation, and stress as a result. When you stop fighting the tide, you'll experience peace at life's ebb and flow.

3. How would loosening your expectations allow you to enjoy whatever shows up in life? What would it be like to see life's events as a gift to be unwrapped? Some are not a hit, some are okay, and some are beyond your wildest dreams. The less rigidly you define what a present should look like, the more surprised and thrilled you'll be with even the smallest gift.

FEAR

Until a few years ago, fear dominated my life. It colored—or stained, depending on how you look at it—virtually all major decisions.

I don't mean the concrete fear that results from real and imminent danger, like a roaring tiger that is poised to attack. Our bodies and minds are hardwired to go into fight-or-flight mode when something like this happens, and thank God, because that hardwiring can mean the difference between life and death.

The fear that dominated my life was abstract fear, which triggers the same physical and mental chemical reactions as concrete fear but is based on a perceived or imaginary threat, not something real or imminent. This kind of fear is a reaction to something hypothetical, something that could happen but is not, in fact, happening right here, right now.

Most people experience abstract fear on a daily basis. It's so common that we've become conditioned to believe it's normal. The problem is that abstract fear is the one thing standing between us and the life we want to create for ourselves. Fear like this is not real, and yet we let it hijack our dreams.

In this chapter, we'll look at how fear shows up and how you can take action to slay that imaginary dragon.

EVER-PRESENT FEAR

When I chose to go to business school, I didn't really want to go to business school. I wanted to be a success, to have a thriving career, and to make my mark while earning lots and lots of money. I wanted all of those things because I—my ego—needed validation. My choice to go to business school was made out of fear of not having all those things, of not being enough.

When I left GE and went into business for myself, many people applauded me for taking this risk and pursuing my dream. They thought I was such a maverick and a courageous person, which my ego loved hearing. Little did they know, I was shaking in my boots with doubt and fear.

My life, and the many twists and turns it has taken to get me where I am today, reads like a crazy novel. On the surface, I did have the chutzpah to choose that kind of life, but underneath that very thin veneer of bravado was a guy gripped by fear: fear of failing, fear of not being the best, fear of not being important, fear of not making the most money, fear of not being rich, fear of not being successful (whatever the heck that means), fear of not looking good, fear of not fitting in, fear of not being loved, fear of my father not being proud of me, and the list goes on. These fears fueled my case of never enoughitis and made me relentless in my pursuit of seeking more money, more power, more recognition, more validation, and more stuff. I got completely lost on the never-ending carousel of always seeking more.

In recent years, I have experienced many setbacks and failures, including the end of my marriage, the loss of my businesses, and the loss of millions of dollars. At times, I doubted I would ever find my way out of the freefall the universe had thrown me into. I was consumed with fear, terrorized by the thought of losing everything. Only when I hit rock bottom, feeling completely empty and deflated and having absolutely no idea where to go or what to do next, did I finally surrender to faith.

FAITH, THE POLAR OPPOSITE OF FEAR

The word *faith* comes from the Old French word *feid*, meaning "faith, belief, trust, confidence, pledge." It's often used when describing religion or the supernatural: people have faith in God or refer to the religion they practice as their faith.

The very essence of faith, however, is believing—I would say surrendering, even—to something far larger than oneself in the absence of any tangible evidence or proof. In terms of polarity, fear can be described as the belief in the worst possible outcome without any real or concrete evidence that it will indeed happen, whereas faith can be described as the belief in the best possible outcome, again without any real or concrete evidence that it will come to pass. As you work on awareness and being conscious of your thoughts and beliefs, you realize that you can choose to move from one pole (fear) to the other (faith).

I am clearly a slow learner.

It took me forty-seven years to come to this awareness and to consciously start choosing faith over fear. I have by no means fully slayed the dragon. However, when I catch myself slipping into fear, I know now how to course-correct and get myself back to faith.

The first step in moving toward faith is simply to catch yourself feeling abstract fear. This awareness alone is huge. In truth, fear is easy to catch once you pay attention because your body will tell you, loud and very clear, when you are experiencing it. I don't have to describe what fear feels like; you know it like the back of your hand.

The next step is asking yourself what is triggering that fear. Instead of running from it or fighting it, examine your fear. Lean into it, and you will get more clarity around its source. Fair warning: this process will be uncomfortable. There's absolutely nothing comfortable about digging, delving, and diving into fear. You will encounter massive resistance from your ego or the imaginary construct of the self. That's right: the *imaginary* construct of the self will resist the *imaginary* threat you are experiencing.

In a nutshell, fear and the feeling of the self being threatened are just bullshit stories created by your mind. If you can grasp that truth, you're halfway home.

Fear typically shows up as some form of resistance, like procrastination, doubt, worry, or anxiety. It may feel uncomfortable, but this resistance can be your best friend. As soon as you encounter internal resistance, it's time to listen.

Resistance is a very important signpost. It's like a stop sign telling you to pause and go within, to examine and delve into this resistance. Ask yourself, "What is this resistance all about? What is it telling me? Why is this coming up for me?"

Don't dwell too long in the research lab, however, because you have to keep moving through the resistance (read: fear). This is where the magic is. Growth is uncomfortable. If you're not uncomfortable, you're not growing. Growth happens when you lean into the resistance and embrace the discomfort of examining your fear triggers. As you make this practice a central theme of your life, you will feel alive, more so than ever before.

As you seek more growth and expansion, you'll also get hooked on seeking discomfort, knowing that the discomfort is simply a doorway to the magic. Think about your own life. Where have you seen this truth? When have you been uncomfortable and slayed a dragon or two?

We live in a world and culture where we do everything in our power to avoid being uncomfortable. We don't try to be comfortable; we actually do our utmost to not be uncomfortable. We also live in a world where we usually judge any failure as bad. Thomas Edison famously said, "I didn't fail. I just found 10,000 ways how not to do it," but we've mostly lost this outlook today.

Like all fear, fear of failure shows up as resistance in the form of procrastination, doubt, worry, or anxiety. To help put your fear in this area to rest, remember this: if you learn something from a failure, whatever that failure might be, you can't actually fail at anything in life. You either succeed or learn, and learning to reframe failure like this is a powerful way to take all the venom (fear) out of failure.

When I hit rock bottom, I surrendered to the notion that I am allowed to fail and that I will still be whole and enough on the other side. I didn't need someone else to give me the liberty to fail. I needed to give myself this freedom at a deep soul level. When I surrendered, fear dissolved like an imaginary soap bubble burst by the gentlest touch of a finger.

Fear is the absence of faith. As darkness cannot exist in the abundance of light, fear cannot exist in the abundance of faith. But while darkness is the absence of light, light is not the absence of darkness. Light is real, but darkness is not. It is an absence, only. Whenever you find yourself engulfed by the darkness of fear, move to the other pole to find some light. Even the smallest, dimmest ray of light will soften the overwhelming feeling of total darkness. And the more light you let in, the softer the darkness becomes until it serves only as a reminder to keep the light on.

SLAY THE DRAGON OF FEAR

One of my favorite books is *How to Stop Worrying and Start Living* by Dale Carnegie. Originally published in 1948, this book is as relevant and useful today as when it was first published. It is a nonspiritual text that can relay very deep meaning and purpose. If life is about suffering, as the Buddha stated, Carnegie's book is all about alleviating the inevitable suffering that life hands us.

Two techniques from Carnegie's book have become instrumental in helping me slay my dragons. The first is related to what James

Altucher (another highly recommended author and podcaster) calls "time travel," or our tendency to live in the past and the future rather than the present. In the absolute present moment—the right now—fear does not exist. Right here, right now, in this instant, fear cannot live. Fear can live in the future and, to some extent, in the past, but in the absolute now, there's no fear.

The next time you are overcome by fear and worry, try this "time travel" exercise from Dale Carnegie. Imagine you are an ocean liner that has a "future" bulkhead and a "past" bulkhead. The bridge on top is now, or today. Imagine closing the heavy metal bulkhead doors that separate and compartmentalize the future bulkhead and the past bulkhead from the bridge. Once you've closed these heavy-duty doors, you can go about your business, doing what you need to (and can) do, right here, right now.

You may think you have control over your life, but that's all an illusion. What you can control is what you do right now. That's it. By closing off the future and past, this exercise anchors you in the now and gets you off the rollercoaster time travel ride of worries and fears that you're projecting onto the past or future.

The second technique is what Carnegie refers to as the Carrier method or rules. This powerful exercise revolves around taking three simple steps whenever you encounter a challenging or difficult situation:

1. Ask yourself, "What's the worst that can happen?" Literally seek to quantify the very worst that could possibly happen. For instance, "I could go bankrupt," or "She might leave me,"

or "I could lose my job." The point is to anchor at the bottom your worst possible fear.

2. Fully accept this worst possible outcome. Lean into it and totally, unconditionally accept this result as if it has already happened.

3. Single-mindedly focus on how or what you can do to improve on this worst possible outcome.

This exercise stops the monkey brain from running so many "worst-case," entirely hypothetical scenarios. It stops the mindless worrying about what might happen. It allows you to focus all your energy on doing what you can right now, in this very moment, to improve on the worst-case outcome you have already accepted. By accepting that worst-case outcome, you are surrendering, which is an act of faith. As I described earlier, the vice grip of fear is released at the very moment you surrender into faith.

In this life, we all have dragons to slay, even after we gain awareness about the true nature of fear. I am no different from you. I have good days, and I have bad days. I still encounter fear. The only difference may be that when fear shows up, I now welcome it in. I bring it closer so I can examine it. I lean into it and feel it permeate my entire body, notice how it shallows my breath and raises my heart rate. Then I go into fucking savage mode.

I picture myself as a samurai, a spiritual warrior of sorts, fully prepared and willing to die for the cause. I will myself to lean into the discomfort, to use all the tools and techniques I have accumulated, and I go after the dragon with a vengeance.

There are days I am so scared I have tremors up my spine. I cry if I have to and scream if I must. I don't care if I look like a fool because I am slaying my dragon, and in this warfare, it doesn't matter how you look or what way you get through it. All that matters is that you get to the other side.

As you move from chaos to order—as you reach the other side and crawl up the riverbank to rest on dry land—you will find that there wasn't a dragon to start with. It was all bullshit, a total fiction of your imagination. But don't worry. You are still a samurai for making it to this side of the river.

YOUR TURN

1. Where and how does fear show up in your life? What are you not doing that you know you should do or want to do? Chances are that fear is what's holding your back.

2. If you had no fear, what would you do? Everything you desire in life, the dream life you envision, is right behind your fears.

3. Once you define your fears, examine them closely. Are they real, concrete fears, or are they abstract, hypothetical fears that are not happening in the here and now?

GROWTH

When I first embarked on my spiritual journey, I had concluded that my old life of pursuing success, validation, and recognition was devoid of meaning, so I looked for a new purpose. I searched for something grandiose, like solving world hunger, but I soon learned this was simply another display of my egoic mind, now projecting itself on something that sounded spiritual and lofty instead of lucrative. It was more never enoughitis cutely disguised in an angelic-sounding mission.

In February 2017, I traveled to Holland to visit my father, who was dying of Parkinson's disease. By this point, my father's mental condition had deteriorated considerably. As I sat with this once accomplished and intelligent businessman who was now on the threshold of passing over to the other side, I realized that death is the great equalizer. All that we accomplish or accumulate in this life is of no value in the final hour. The special moments, the experiences, love, and how you evolved during your lifetime are what matters.

When my dad finally passed a month later, something in me shifted, and I let go of the notion that I needed to find some grandiose purpose. I then understood what I had read in the ancient wisdom traditions: that our one and only purpose in life is to grow.

OUR ONE PURPOSE

As discussed in the last chapter, growing is a bitch. It requires an uncomfortable journey into the abyss of the unknown. Whether you're learning to write, skate, make love, or develop patience, if you're venturing into new territory, you will experience discomfort on the way to growth.

At the same time, however, growth is an integral part of life. In fact, our only real purpose in life is to grow. Think about it: each one of us is born a small and defenseless ball of consciousness, and over the course of our lives, we evolve and grow into the most ferocious, powerful, and ruthless creature on planet earth.

At birth, our underdeveloped brain and senses leave us completely defenseless. Our survival depends entirely on the loving hands and nurturing care of our parents. Over time, the brain and body grow to show a seemingly infinite potential to become ever smarter and wiser. We develop spiritual insights, wisdom, and faith that the baby we were born as couldn't comprehend.

Yet in spite of that growth and how uncomfortable it has to be, we naturally seek comfort. One of our mind's main tasks is to make sure we're comfortable, and that voice inside our head will tell us stories to keep us from trying things that bring discomfort. To grow, we need to learn how to ignore those voices and see discomfort as a friend leading the way to the arena where magic is created. When you evolve and grow, the entire universe evolves and grows because everything and everyone is all connected. Your gain is a gain for everyone. We all win, and that is pure magic.

To accomplish your one purpose in life, you have to lean into discomfort. As you do, you push your limits, you expand, and you become the best version of yourself. In addition, as you move those boundaries, you touch the lives of others, as you have now made room and illuminated the path for others to follow you.

Discomfort is your best friend; welcome it in.

THE IMPORTANCE OF MINDSET

I believe mindset is often overlooked by those who embark on the spiritual journey as if our mental side (read: mind) is the enemy of being heart-centered (read: love) or soul-centered (read: spirit). I don't see it that way. The body, mind, heart, and soul are all interconnected and interdependent. They each have a unique role to play and collectively make up the whole. For the whole to grow, all areas need to evolve and grow, or the weakest link will limit the potential of the whole. We must develop the mind right alongside the body, heart, and soul.

In her bestselling book *Mindset: The New Psychology of Success*, Stanford Psychologist Carol S. Dweck synthesizes the findings of her twenty years of research into the power of our beliefs, both conscious and unconscious, and how changing even the simplest of them can have a profound impact on nearly every aspect of our lives.

According to Dweck, one of the most basic beliefs we carry about ourselves has to do with our personality and shows up as either a fixed or a growth mindset.

A "fixed mindset" assumes that our character, intelligence, and creative ability are static givens that we can't change in any meaningful way, and that success is the affirmation of our inherent intelligence—an assessment of how those givens measure up against an equally fixed standard. As a result, striving for success and avoiding failure becomes a way of maintaining the sense of being smart or skilled.

A "growth mindset," on the other hand, views character traits, intelligence, and creative ability as dynamic and changeable. It thrives on challenge and sees failure not as evidence of unintelligence but as a heartening springboard for growth and for stretching our existing abilities.

Out of these two mindsets, which we manifest from a very early age, springs a great deal of our behavior, our relationship with success and failure in both professional and personal contexts, and ultimately our capacity for happiness. Although we are born with a tendency toward one mindset or the other, that mindset is not permanent. You can vacillate between mindsets, and it's important to be aware of which one you're adopting in any given moment or situation.

Knowing that your mindset is pliable and malleable is downright empowering in itself. Even if you are hardwired with a fixed mindset, being aware of that mindset allows you to consciously rewire yourself. You can yank out all the thoughts, ideas, or beliefs that no longer serve you, then consciously create and reprogram your mind with thoughts, ideas, and beliefs that empower you to be the best version of you.

As with all growth, this kind of change involves discomfort, lots of it. Some of this old wiring doesn't really want to go. Some of it was soldered in place with such a tight bond that it seems impossible to remove, but it's not. All effort to rewire your mindset develops your willpower. Every bit of progress, of pushing your limits out a little further into what was previously unchartered territory, will make you stronger, more determined, and more resilient.

David Goggins, author of the highly recommended book, *Can't Hurt Me*, epitomizes another aspect of mindset: immense mental fortitude or toughness created by relentlessly pursuing mastery of the mind. The mind is weak and will always direct you toward the path of least resistance. The egoic mind doesn't want to grow because it fundamentally likes what it knows. The unknown and uncertainty are the mind's worst enemy, and it will do everything in its power to steer clear of both.

The question then becomes, "Who is in control?"

Who is the master of the mind? When you are awakened, you—the observer of your thoughts and beliefs—are in control, not your ego. Any time you make a conscious decision, you are the master. Any time you let the ego and its (quite possibly outdated) automatic programs run the show, you allow the egoic mind to be the master, and you, in turn, become its servant. What David Goggins's book aptly illustrates is that the mind is more than a worthy enemy. Mastering our mind requires the vigilance and persistence of a true warrior who understands deep down that individual battles might be lost from time to time, but the true victory is in winning the war. The secret is to keep getting up. Remember, your sole purpose is to grow.

OWN THE POWER TO GROW

Look around you. Size up your entire life. Where you are today, all the things you have and don't have, is the summation of every little decision—conscious or unconscious—you have made. Nothing is random, and nothing happens by accident.

In general, we like to claim credit for all the "good" things in our lives and blame all the "bad" things on something external, whether that's a person, a natural disaster, or just bad luck. However, until you own your whole life, good and bad, you can't step into the power to change it. Until that moment, you are outsourcing your life's destiny to fate.

To the ego, it doesn't seem fair that you "own" that lost job because of the factory that closed down or the Ponzi scheme that wiped out your pension savings, but you need to own it anyway. Ownership is about taking responsibility not for what happened, but the acceptance that it happened. Without acceptance that something happened, we cannot heal and move beyond the pain it caused us. You are responsible for your life. You are responsible for fulfilling your purpose—for growing into the very best version of yourself. Quit having pity for yourself or looking for excuses. Look in the mirror. Take ownership and be accountable to yourself.

Taking ownership does not suggest that you are the *cause* of everything in your life. I am not arguing that you consciously created every circumstance in your life. Taking ownership is not so much about who or what created your life as it is about who owns it. If something is part of your life, you own it. If you don't own a part of your life—even the job loss or the unjustifiable abuse—you're stuck in victimhood and won't be able to heal it. You'll leave yourself powerless to grow and change.

The moment you step into unconditional ownership of the good, the bad, and the ugly, you claim and create the very power that will help you shape a much more deliberate, consciously created world centered around becoming the best version of you.

In the years leading up to my divorce in late 2017, I embarked on my spiritual journey because I was searching for my answers—a way off the never enoughitis carousel, really—but I was still stuck in victimhood. Deep down, I still blamed much of my emptiness on outside factors: If my wife was a certain way, my marriage wouldn't feel so lonely. If my business was going better, I wouldn't feel so dissatisfied. And the list goes on. I didn't fully own any of it yet. It wasn't until I went into therapy after my divorce that I grew the balls to accept that I own every single piece of my own life—all the good, all the bad, and especially all the ugly. In that moment, I slowly but surely reclaimed my power.

Today, that ownership has evolved to an even higher level because not only do I own and take responsibility for every aspect of my life, I can also see how life is always working for my greatest growth, my greatest prosperity, and my greatest evolution. Accepting this involves pure faith, total trust in the benevolence of this universe, and that there's a far greater intelligence at work behind the scenes of which I simply have no comprehension. I have seen that Infinite Intelligence at work too many times now, in all its mysterious ways, so I can no longer do anything but trust it fully.

DELAYED GRATIFICATION

The ability to defer instant gratification is perhaps the single greatest attributor to success in life—success of any kind, not just financial or material. We live in a world where the average attention span has been reduced to whatever fits on the screen of a phone and can be consumed in mere seconds. From early childhood, people are being trained and conditioned to enjoy quick and instant fixes.

Growth is slow. Growth comes with setbacks. Growth comes in fits and spurts and requires effort and commitment. The goal is not depriving yourself for the sake of creating artificial hardships but deferring instant gratification in service of growth.

Imagine what superpowers you would have if you exercised this muscle so much that it became second nature. Here's how delayed gratification would play out in the following scenarios: When you're negotiating your next pay package, you accept a lower base salary with a richer bonus potential or even equity options, knowing you have far more upside than securing a higher base. When your friends are lost in the city life, you decide to study for exams. When your friends blow their paycheck on beer and cheap dates, you set aside money for the trip you want to take. When your own sexual satisfaction is *not* your primary focus, you cultivate control over your orgasm so you can be a more generous lover.

In all scenarios, training the muscle of deferring instant gratifi-cation is a gift you give yourself. If you're a parent like me, it's quite possibly the single most valuable lesson you can pass on to your kids to set them up for epic success in all areas of their life.

SEEK HELP IN YOUR GROWTH

As I mentioned before, growth doesn't always come easily or nat-urally, and more often than not, it's a struggle—a worthwhile struggle but a struggle nonetheless. Sometimes you are so stuck in your ways that it's difficult to take a step back and look at your-self honestly and objectively. Sometimes the wounds are so deep and visceral, healing needs help from another modality. I am a huge proponent of getting outside help. Sometimes you just need someone who can hold space for you or provide the insight you need or perspective you're not seeing. With the guidance of your intuition, seek out psychologists, psychiatrists, healers, life coaches, guides, gurus, or others who can assist you on your path.

At other times, healing can be facilitated or even accelerated with the help of Mother Earth, for instance, through plant medicines like ayahuasca and other forms of traditional shamanic medicine like *Bufo alvarius*. I am not advertising these medicines or arguing their validity, but I will share that these have been instrumental in breaking the spiritual path wide open for me. All of our journeys are different, but I would be remiss to not mention my intense gratitude for the shamans and medicine men and women who have served me on my path of growth.

Remember, your purpose is to grow—nothing else.

YOUR TURN

1. Are you endlessly searching for your grand purpose? Do you often wonder what your mission in life is or why you are here? What if your purpose is simply to grow and evolve? Look deeply into this question and ask yourself if that demystifies everything.

2. Do you view your experiences as growth opportunities? If you don't currently, what would happen if you shifted your perspective in this way? You might see every experience as another piece of the puzzle that is your life.

3. Are you committed to keeping a growth mindset, to always be evolving, to staying curious and intellectually hungry? Challenging yourself in this way will keep life juicy and adventurous. Accept and embrace the fact that growth comes with growing pains. This is the natural way as we venture into the unknown and push our own limits and boundaries.

RADICAL HONESTY

One of the main reasons my marriage failed is that I was completely incapable of sharing my feelings. I was afraid to be honest about my deepest fears and worries, my depression, and more, so I wore a mask to hide what was really going on. As a result, I shut Cara out, and we became strangers. To numb the pain, I turned to alcohol, drugs, pharmaceuticals, and later debauchery, but I was still miserable and lost.

In summer 2017, as part of my haphazard search for answers, I attended a weeklong retreat in Rancho la Puerta that powerfully changed my perspective on honesty. By that point, Cara and I were already heading for divorce, so I didn't implement radical honesty to save my marriage, but I did continue to explore this concept when I entered therapy a few months later. As I did so, I slowly took off my mask and allowed my heart to open, and I have never been the same since.

In this chapter, I'll discuss some of the key concepts of radical honesty as well as the rules that can help you create a safe space to implement it in your relationships.

WHAT IS RADICAL HONESTY?

Radical honesty is just what it sounds like: absolute, unfiltered, unedited honesty about thoughts, feelings, fears, dreams, and more. It is a very close cousin of authenticity.

Radical honesty will revolutionize all your relationships, especially your most intimate ones, but it starts with radical honesty with yourself. The more brutally honest you are able to get with yourself, without any dilution of self-love, the more radical honesty will naturally spill over into your relationships and catapult your personal growth into the stratosphere.

As you incorporate radical honesty into your daily life and overall being, you will find the expression of your authentic self becomes more natural and in sync with who you truly are without the masks and layers of social or cultural programming. And people will notice. People are naturally drawn to, even magnetized by, people who are authentic. As you shed the layers of social conditioning and the various masks you hide behind, your authentic self cannot help but shine through. You will become more vibrant and radiant, your energy will light up the room, and your gentle touch or warm embrace will become healing to others.

You likely know this to be true because you have been around or at least heard about people like this. Maybe not that often, but occasionally you come in contact with a person whose vibration of authenticity is simply captivating. That can be you. You are destined to be your authentic self. It simply requires that you become totally and radically honest with yourself and all you touch. Strip out all the layers of bullshit, clean up all the gunk, and heal your wounds. We all have our own variety of these things, but the path to true authenticity is identical for all of us.

CREATING A SAFE PLACE

We are all soft, mushy, and incredibly sensitive and vulnerable beings. I don't care what mask you choose to wear and show the world; you are vulnerable. So many things hurt us and our feelings. The smallest unintended words can cause irreparable harm, even lifelong trauma that shapes the trajectory of our lives.

As children, we lack the filter or cognizance to guard our hearts and minds against hurtful words. We're like sponges in those early developmental years, soaking up others' comments as if they're absolute truth. Later, we develop a filter, and we have a little more conscious control over what goes into our beliefs about ourselves and the world. Even still, we remain highly sensitive and vulnerable because our mind (read: ego) takes everything literally and personally. As a result, we naturally develop a moat around our feelings so that we don't get hurt. We don't like that uncomfortable feeling, so we do whatever we can to protect ourselves from experiencing it. (Though, as you know now, discomfort is the signpost that growth is ahead, so we should really lean in.)

To communicate openly and freely, to genuinely share your innermost feelings, wishes, desires, and fears, you have to first feel safe—not just sort of safe but completely, 100 percent safe. It doesn't matter how spiritually advanced you are: if you are afraid you might get hurt, you cannot—and will not—express yourself fully and unapologetically. This is simply human nature. We are not wired to seek pain and hurt, especially not emotional or mental pain, which is far more difficult to endure than physical pain. We are wired to seek pleasure and safety.

To allow radical honesty to emerge, you have to create a safe place where all superheroes can hang their cape at the door, all masks can come off, and people can share their raw and unfiltered truths. They can share the way the world occurs to them, their reality, feelings, emotions, kinks, preferences, wishes, dreams, and fears. A safe place is where real communication, or radical honesty, can take place.

So, what creates a safe place? A safe place is anchored by three principles, the sacred rules of engagement:

1. No judgment
2. No repercussions
3. Unconditional love

To establish a safe place between two or more people (yes, you can also do this in groups small and large), you have to talk through these rules and have full commitment from all who are going to be part of the safe place. It's critically important that everyone energetically "holds" a safe place. If you spring a leak by violating one of these rules, it will not work. A safe place requires total commitment from all involved.

The first rule, no judgment, provides each person the confidence that whatever they share will not be judged as good, bad, or anything in between. The others hearing what is shared need to view it as that person's reality, how they see and experience the world based on the life they've lived up to that moment. Humans are prewired to judge, but as the recipient of radical honesty, your job is to simply listen, not judge.

The second rule, no repercussions, provides each person the assurance that whatever is shared will not be used against them at a later time. It is human nature to hold back if we suspect someone will use what we share to hurt us later, which defeats the purpose of creating a safe place to open up.

This second rule is crucial. As the recipient of someone's radical honesty, your commitment is that there will absolutely be no repercussions. You might bring up a topic in a loving and supportive way, but you can never bring up and use something shared against that person. If you do, the sacred pact will be violated, and that trust will never be fully restored.

The third rule, unconditional love, encapsulates the first two. The entire safe place is held together in and by unconditional love. Before someone engages in radical honesty, they must know beyond a shadow of a doubt that the others will love them no matter what they share.

Unconditional love is not the silly telenovela bullshit we see on TV or even what most glossy-eyed newlyweds believe they signed up for. Unconditional love goes far deeper than romantic love. It is an impregnable force that is without any boundaries or limitations. Unconditional love is Nelson Mandela choosing to love his guards during an unjustified twenty-seven years in captivity on Robben Island. Unconditional love is choosing to love your enemies, knowing that they are merely living their truth from their current level of consciousness. Unconditional love is choosing the excruciating heartbreak of letting your girlfriend go because you know that's what she needs right now. Unconditional love is the glue that holds a safe place together.

In the safe space I created in my last relationship, my partner and I used the code word RH to signal when we were sharing something that is not to be judged or used against us. If I said "This is an RH"—or if she said it to me—we knew that what followed was something personal, something deep and intimate, something said in the protective confines of the safe place we created by mutual commitment.

To engage in radical honesty and incorporate this into your life, you have to be willing to be naked—to be exposed and vulnerable, which may sound uncomfortable, but the rewards are so worth it. (More on vulnerability in the next chapter.)

Radical honesty can bring a richness and depth of communication to your life that you would have never thought possible. In a romantic relationship, this can dial up your love connection and even intimacy to stratospheric levels. Nothing will blow open the door to divine ecstasy and bliss like the ability to deeply communicate with your partner about your innermost dreams and desires.

But here's the catch: this stuff is not easy. Complete and radical honesty requires a high level of awareness, mindfulness, and integrity. The slightest change in your energy can freeze your partner and lock up the whole safe place. Women tend to welcome radical honesty more than men unless they have their own wounds that need to be healed before they're ready for that level of vulnerability. Many men aren't used to or comfortable sharing their deepest feelings, let alone truly intimate ones. They often do well to find or create a men's group, as it's often easier to start this practice within a group of male friends.

At some point, you will find yourself able to communicate in a radically honest way without the formal establishment of a safe place (although you would still occasionally use it, for instance, with your most intimate relationship, in which you are most exposed). At this mastery level, you don't need a safe place commitment from others because you are at total self-love. You don't need to be guaranteed "no judgment" because others' judgment no longer touches you. It doesn't matter what others think of you because you know you're whole. You are not concerned about repercussions because nothing can be used against you, as there is no longer a you (read: ego) to trigger. And finally, you don't *need* someone else's unconditional love because you love yourself (and everyone else) unconditionally.

I am well on my way, but I still have work to do on my way to total mastery, but I have embraced radical honesty in every aspect of my life, and I am forever grateful for these lessons Lisa Nichols introduced me to.

YOUR TURN

1. Ask yourself, "What part of me is not fully expressed? Where am I holding back?" You might be holding back different things in different relationships, but each part we're not fully expressing is where we've still got some sort of mask on.

2. Examine why you're not fully expressing or sharing some part of yourself. What do you fear losing by sharing? What could you gain from sharing? Use journaling to crystallize your thoughts around these questions. Usually, the real answers are a few layers down.

3. What relationship do you value enough to start being radically honest? Create a safe place using the rules described earlier. Enroll the other person (or people) into the possibility of what can be gained by deepening the relationship. A safe place can only be created when both people fully enroll; otherwise, the container will spring a leak and likely damage the relationship. It's challenging to recover from a trust that's been violated, so go about this very intentionally, and you'll soon start seeing your relationships deepen and strengthen.

VULNERABILITY

If you are anything like me, the word *vulnerability* makes you cringe. Actually, *cringe* doesn't come close to describing the depth of dislike, denial, and repulsion that word used to trigger in me.

Why do we react this way? I think it's because we misunderstand the concept of vulnerability. We associate it with weakness and being soft when, in fact, it is the exact opposite.

I was first exposed to a different view of vulnerability when I stumbled on Brené Brown's books in 2016 and 2017 (she also has a must-see TED Talk on the subject). While I recognized truth in what I read, it wasn't until I started dropping the idea that I had to be a "certain somebody" that I could start incorporating the ideas into my life.

In this chapter, I have liberally borrowed from Brown's work, especially *Braving the Wilderness* and *Daring Greatly*, as she's been such a valuable teacher for me. We will look at what vulnerability is, how fear of vulnerability shows up, and how it causes us to live a shadow life that is safe, boring, and ultimately unfulfilling.

THE PATH TO JOY

Where radical honesty requires us to be vulnerable, vulnerability is essential to fostering true connection, which is arguably as fundamental to health and well-being as breathing oxygen. Vulnerability is also the pathway to getting real with yourself and aligning with your authentic self.

Just as we are wired for comfort, we also want to belong, so anything that exposes us to possible rejection is terrifying. Even the slightest misspoken or unintended words by a stranger or a close friend or loved one has the power to lacerate and crush us. You have to be enormously courageous and strong to consciously allow yourself to be exposed like that. In this sense, vulnerability is the exact opposite of weakness.

Nothing about being vulnerable is comfortable. The icky gut feeling, sweaty palms, shallow breathing, and slightly raised pulse—it's just not a pleasant experience. But as you've probably seen by now, the good stuff in life comes from embracing discomfort and moving through it.

In some ways, vulnerability is part of the fabric of life: when you lean in for the first kiss, when you tell your girl you love her for the first time, when you risk losing a friend over something you have to tell them, even when you interview for the job you really want. Any time there's a possibility of rejection, dismissal, or of being hurt, you are vulnerable.

Why do we choose to put ourselves through the discomfort in these situations? Because it's also the path to experiencing all the love, joy, happiness, and bliss that life has to offer.

On the other side of vulnerability lies the magic stuff of life. A sense of love, joy, gratitude, and happiness all open up to you when you're willing to be vulnerable. When you close yourself off, when you guard yourself emotionally, you also dial down your ability to experience these emotions. Yes, you might limit the possible hurt, but you also limit the potential joy or pleasure. It's like making love with a condom: sure, it's pretty good, but it could be so much better. If you have your sights on epic, if you want to feel deeply all that life has to offer, if you want to walk on air once in a while and experience truly exuberant joy, and if you want to live life to the fullest, then you have to embrace the risk of being hurt.

To truly love deeply, to get totally lost in it, is to also risk heartbreak. For the girl who caught your attention to go out on a first date, you have to ask and risk being turned down. To get that job you've been dreaming about, you have to apply, which means you'll risk not getting it. That shot you'd like to have at entrepreneurship and perhaps unimaginable success and even wealth come with the risk that the venture will fail.

To play the game of life, you have to get into the arena. To get into the arena, you have to be willing to be vulnerable. Most people are not willing, so they stay on the outside looking in. They talk a good bit about it, maybe dabble a toe in the water, but most people can't handle the discomfort, so they regress into comfort. They stand by as others step into the arena and often are the first ones to criticize the people playing the game full out, especially when they stumble or fall flat on their face.

The ones in the arena typically don't criticize. They will encourage you, help you back up when you fall, and cheer you on as you slay your dragons, for they know the balls it took to get into the arena in the first place. That's just the way life works: only those who get into the arena, who are willing to fail and experience setbacks, will ultimately win by experiencing life to its fullest. Only those who get into the arena, over and over again, taste the sweet indulgence of fully and unreservedly making love to life.

A NEW RELATIONSHIP WITH FAILURE

As discussed earlier, many people have a screwed-up relationship with failure. We attach judgment to failure or breakdown, viewing it as a bad thing when that's not the true essence of a breakdown at all. A breakdown is a lesson, that's all. To have a breakdown, you have to first venture into the arena of life. You have to make a move, take action, endeavor, and by doing so, inevitably take a risk that the situation might not work out. However small or big that risk might be, taking a risk requires you to be vulnerable. It's always safest, as well as easier and more comfortable, to just stand by and take no risk at all.

Sometimes the lesson is obvious; sometimes it's not. Sometimes you have to look a little harder or let some time pass so you can connect the dots in the rearview mirror. The truth is you can only connect the dots through the rearview mirror. Some dots might be visible looking at the present and future, but most aren't, so don't get frustrated when the answers or reasons aren't immediately obvious. There's no way to grasp things that haven't happened yet because there are infinite possibilities. Stop trying to control the future; it's a complete waste of energy. You can't control life; it's going to unfold exactly as needs to, in perfect order, no matter what happens.

Instead, fully embrace any breakdown and see it merely as an indicator that you need to learn, grow, or pivot, or that it was a door not meant for you to open.

If you live life fully, you will experience a lot of breakdowns. Get used to it. The more breakdowns, the better, because that means you're probably experiencing many highs as well. Ups and downs, chaos and order, good and bad, successes and breakdowns—polarity will show itself as a common thread throughout your life story. So fully embrace a breakdown. Dig into it to find the lesson because therein lies the silver lining. Breakdowns are beautiful. Welcome them in as a sign that you are living life exactly like you are fucking supposed to. We're here to grow, learn, and experience life to the fullest, and part of that is breakdowns. A life without breakdowns is a life stripped of all the highs and excitement as well. It's a muted and dulled-down version of what's possible. When we are unwilling to be vulnerable and embrace the discomfort that comes with it, we rob ourselves of all the juicy stuff life has to offer.

STEP INTO THE ARENA

Once you do step into the arena and embrace vulnerability, you will find that the deepening of your relations and connections—the expansion of joy, creativity, love, and your sense of belonging—is intoxicating. After a while, you won't be able to imagine showing up in any other way because you've now tasted life's nectar in an unadulterated way.

The beautiful paradox of vulnerability is that the moment you truly embrace vulnerability, you actually stop being vulnerable in the same way that you cannot kick in a door that is already open. The moment you allow yourself to be truly vulnerable is the very moment you decide you are enough. Of course, you still want things to go the way you hope and wish, but if they don't, you're no longer crushed or devastated because you know, deep down inside, that whatever rejection or dismissal you just experienced doesn't change your worth as a person. Your soul always *is*. Only the ego gets hurt or insulted.

I used to vehemently reject and dismiss the entire notion of vulnerability, as I was under the illusion being vulnerable meant I was weak or soft. Vulnerability has now become one of my superpowers, and I passionately embrace it—and the jitters it gives me whenever I do—because I know those jitters are only a sign that I am truly being my authentic self. And chances are, magic is right ahead.

I have never loved deeper, been more passionate, radiated more joy, or experienced more connection and belonging than I do these days because I have learned to embrace vulnerability, which has allowed me to step into the arena of life over and over again. I still stumble and fall sometimes, and I still experience the occasional rejection or hurt, but that doesn't stop me anymore because I also get to fully experience the peaks. My heart is lighter as I stay true to myself because I'm no longer wearing masks and trying to be something I'm not.

I am so passionate about vulnerability that I have Theodore Roosevelt's famous "Man in the Arena" speech framed in my home as a daily reminder to err on the side of discomfort just so I can live life to the fullest:

It's not the critic who counts;

Not the man who points out how the strong man stumbles or

where the doer of deeds could have done them better.

The credit belongs to the man who is actually in the arena,

whose face is marred by dust and sweat and blood;

who strives valiantly; who errs, who comes short again and again,

because there is no effort without error and shortcoming;

but who does actually strive to do the deeds;

who knows great enthusiasms, the great devotions;

who spends himself in a worthy cause; who at the best knows in
the end

the triumph of high achievement and who at the worst, if he fails,

at least fails while daring greatly.

So that his place shall never be with those cold and timid souls

who neither know victory or defeat.

YOUR TURN

1. Do you hold back because you are scared you might get hurt (or embarrassed or misunderstood or ridiculed or however "hurt" shows up for you)? What are you so afraid of? Will it kill you? Does getting hurt say anything about you? What false stories have you attached to getting hurt that are stopping you from expressing yourself fully and being vulnerable?

2. What's your relationship with failure or breakdowns? Do you relate them to being a failure as a person? Or do you appropriately classify the failure for what it is: an opportunity to learn and evolve?

3. What would you gain from being more vulnerable? How would this make you more resilient, daring, and able to take risks? How would it enable you to reach for those things in life you want but currently can't access because you are unable to embrace vulnerability?

FORGIVENESS

Forgiveness is a noble act of self-love.

Yes, you read that right: to forgive is to be righteously selfish. You might not always deserve to be forgiven, but you always deserve to forgive.

Many of us were taught to think of forgiveness as something that (1) only God (or maybe royalty) can truly bestow upon us, especially as it pertains to our "sins" and/or (2) benefits the redeemed receiver of the forgiveness but not necessarily the benevolent giver.

The fact is, you can forgive without the receiver realizing it; the receiver can even be deceased, and you can still grant forgiveness. That means a burglary victim can forgive her unknown robber. You can forgive your deceased parent. These are just some examples we all know to be true, so why do we generally think of forgiveness in the way we do? Religion is why. Since the advent of Christianity, forgiveness is something we have come to associate with various religious teachings. Forgiveness became something weighty, as in only God can forgive us for our sins, with a huge religious undercurrent, and we totally lost sight of the essence, and maybe more importantly, the healing powers of forgiveness.

In this chapter, we'll look at the rationale behind forgiveness as well as the practice itself.

> "To err is human; to forgive, divine."
>
> —ALEXANDER POPE

THE RATIONALE

Understanding the why of forgiveness starts with remembering two truths:

1. Everything you experience is, by definition, relative truth— your unique point of view is not absolute truth.
2. The act of remembering occurs when we make a story up about what happened.

The events can be relatively objective and indisputable (e.g., "I lost my job"), but the story surrounding those events is a highly subjective interpretation of what actually happened and even more so what it means.

As discussed, our brains are meaning-making machines, and we have an unstoppable urge to assign meaning to each and every thing that happens in our life. When the thing is good in the relative truth that is our viewpoint, we are left with positive emotions or charges, like joy, happiness, and maybe even bliss. However, when what happened is a negative thing from our viewpoint, we are left with negative emotions or charges, like hurt, pain, resentment, or anger.

When we believe we were "wronged" by someone or something, we're actually burdened with toxic negative charges, and they can reverberate until the day we die. Sometimes these negative charges grow louder over time and make us bitter and morose. Carrying negative charges for long periods can compromise your health as well, both physically (e.g., lowering your immune system) and mentally (e.g., depression). In all those ways, unresolved negative charges can become a destructive force in your life, ruining intimate relationships, friendships, and even careers as they fester inside.

How do you neutralize or heal a negative charge? Through forgiveness.

THE PRACTICE

The goal of forgiveness is not to absolve the other person. Forgiveness doesn't mean you condone the wrongdoing or accept their actions or even forget about them—although a nice side effect of forgiveness is often forgetting.

Forgiveness is all about the giver; the receiver is entirely tangential. Forgiveness means you are releasing the negative charges that result from lingering hurt, pain, resentment, and anger. Forgiveness means you are healing yourself from the wound caused by another. We forgive in order to make ourselves whole again.

Now, does the statement "forgiveness is a noble act of *self*-love" start to make sense?

Even though the process leading up to forgiving can often be uncomfortable, as it forces you to relive the pain or hurt that needs to be released, the actual act of forgiving can be comforting, like dropping a huge weight from your shoulder. In addition, the act of forgiving is an act of reclaiming power. Holding on to anger, regret, hatred, or resentment toward someone means you are giving your personal power to that person. Until you choose to forgive, you have a proverbial noose around your neck, held by a person who might not be alive anymore or may be unaware that they wronged you!

The act of forgiveness takes courage and bravery. You have to relinquish your attachment to the hurt, pain, resentment, or anger, which can be very strong, especially if the event was malicious or deeply traumatizing. Forgiving will require that you reach deep down into the deep ocean of love in your heart, past the pain and heartbreak. Just remember that on the other side is liberation and healing from the intense negative charges that may have derailed your life. After all, you are forgiving to heal yourself.

You can know something is the right thing to do for you and still not be able to muster the will to do it. Being deeply steeped in hurt, pain, resentment, or anger can be like quicksand—the more you try to liberate yourself, the more stuck you seem to get. If you find this to be true, it might help to remember some spiritual wisdom that helped me, both in everyday situations and in giving forgiveness: in life, people are doing their best from their current level of consciousness.

Maybe your offender committed something unthinkable, or maybe it was only a small infraction or a few carelessly uttered words. No matter what happened, it might help to remind your-self that the individual did the best they could from where they were in that moment. Hurt people hurt people. Unless you walk a mile in their shoes, you don't know what they endured in life or what brought them to do what they did.

This can be a hard truth to grasp, especially when they do something malicious, but forgiving doesn't mean you're condoning, approving, or justifying the act in any way. Forgiveness is purely about liberating yourself from the pain, hurt, anger, or resentment that's holding you hostage, making the original wrong a life sentence for you until you release it.

To forgive the person and heal your wounds, you might think you need to understand what brought them to that moment. You don't. To forgive, you don't need the person to explain themselves or feel sorry for what they've done. Remember, the recipient of forgiveness is tangential to this practice. The healing that comes through the act of forgiveness is for you.

If the circumstances allow and you feel this will be helpful for your own healing or mending the relationship, forgiveness in person can be very powerful. If you go to the person to extend forgiveness directly to them, you might find that they have no idea that they hurt you and are mortified by the anguish they caused and profusely apologize. Most people don't mean to hurt other people, and most people feel awful when they do.

Perhaps your offender is no longer alive, or perhaps you've lost track of the person, or perhaps you don't even know the person directly at all—an unknown assailant, for instance. Maybe the individual knows what they did and simply is not sorry. In that case, the person is likely still at that same level of consciousness at which they wronged you or has a relative truth—an interesting point of view—that is different than yours.

Whatever the case, the act of forgiveness allows you to heal your wounds and reclaim your personal power. Those healing powers are accessible to you no matter what the offense, no matter how the person currently views the situation, no matter whether the person is even alive. The only requirement is that you forgive the other person. That's it. The offender has zero say in your act of forgiveness. Their acceptance or refusal or denial of your forgiveness will not render it any less healing for your wounds. Forgiveness is you taking control of your life, liberating yourself from any negative charges, and freeing yourself from the enslavement of any past events so you can live free in the now.

Earlier, I mentioned that when my father passed away, many of his old friends told me how my dad constantly talked about my accomplishments—and that I fell apart after learning that he really was proud of me, although he never said so. I thought I had dealt with this deep wound, but my reaction after the funeral showed me I hadn't. Because I hadn't yet forgiven my dad, I still carried many negative charges, including never enoughitis. So much of my behavior and hunger for validation and recognition can be traced back to my relationship with my dad.

After hearing that my father was actually proud of me, I took a step back and started looking at his life as a whole and what made him the person he became. He was born in 1940, and the Nazis occupied the Netherlands a few months after his birth. His dad perished in a Polish Nazi work camp when he was three years old, and he endured the "hunger winter" that resulted when the Nazis confiscated food supplies in still occupied territories, creating severe food scarcity for the local populations. After the war, his now single mom made very little money as a school teacher, so he grew up with scarcity all around him.

Scarcity, more than anything else, shaped him as a person and the man he would ultimately become. No matter how successful he was in his career, which he took to great heights, he always felt poor and was never able to shake his scarcity mentality. To him, life was a fight for survival because that's how he experienced it. He became one tough, stoic motherfucker, as to him, there was no God looking out for him. It was him against the rest of the world, and this is what he set out to teach his sons: to be tough, to be self-reliant, to be tenacious, and most of all, to endure whatever comes your way. Sweet talk and positive encouragement didn't fit into what he wanted to convey to us.

As I started seeing all of this, I could do nothing but thank him. I realized that his lack of expressiveness had nothing to do with me not being good enough. He just didn't know how to share his pride in me, even as he got older and a little milder in his ways. In hindsight, I could see how he prepared me for life and my journey. None of my friends dropped out of college at twenty-one and ventured to the other side of the world. Even though my hard-ass dad immediately cut me off, that didn't stop me because I had jobs since I was five years old, and I knew I would figure out a way to keep my pants up. I did many things for the wrong reasons (never enoughitis!) in my twenties, thirties, and early forties, but I was incredibly self-reliant, tenacious, and tough as fucking nails as I pushed and willed my way to worldly success. Those are my dad's fingerprints all over me. I wouldn't have accomplished what I have if it weren't for the deep wounds he had from his childhood, which he passed on in the way he showed up as a father to me.

Thinking through my dad's history and influence on me finally brought everything full circle, and I had a private forgiveness ceremony where I celebrated his life and all that he did for me, and I finally released the hurt. I've never loved my dad more than I do now. I cherish all that he did to make me the man I've become, and I hold no trace of negative charge anymore. I am whole with him.

HO'OPONOPONO

I am a sucker for sacred and shamanic rituals. I believe that in our fast-paced, urbanized world of concrete and electronics, we have lost our connection with our true essence and nature. Rituals help me slow down and take in the beauty all around.

One of my very favorite sacred wisdom practices is Ho'opono-pono, the indigenous Hawaiian practice of reconciliation and forgiveness. *Ho'o* is a particle used to make an actualizing verb from the noun that follows it. *Ponopono* is defined as "to put right; to put in order or shape, correct, revise, adjust, amend, regulate, arrange, rectify, tidy up, make orderly or neat." Ho'oponopono then means exactly what we have been describing forgiveness to be: an act of healing, of making it right, of becoming whole again.

The modern practice of Ho'oponopono involves repeating a mantra while setting an intention. It is based on the work published by Ihaleakala Hew Len, who believes in taking 100 percent responsibility for everyone's actions, not just for your own. According to Len, if we take complete responsibility for our own life, then we also own everything we see, hear, taste, touch, or in any way experience because it is in our life. In this way, the problem is not with our external reality or what happened; it is with ourselves and what we have called into our lives. Total Responsibility, as described by Hew Len, advocates that everything exists as a projection from inside the human being, which is consistent with ancient wisdom traditions like Buddhism and Taoism.

Against this backdrop, the act of forgiveness can also be seen as forgiving ourselves, for, at some level, we often blame ourselves for things that happen to us. In forgiving the other person, as well as ourselves—which is the ultimate act of self-love—we heal ourselves.

The beauty of Ho'oponopono is that the practice lends itself to directing forgiveness to anyone or anything, including yourself. The mantra is said to have an extremely high frequency (love), which makes it a powerful healing agent.

The Ho'oponopono mantra is as follows:

I am sorry.

Please forgive me.

I love you.

Thank you.

It's said that the order of the sentences is not strict, but the words should be spoken with deep intention. My own adaption of Ho'oponopono is as follows (my intention in parenthesis):

I am sorry (for whatever I have done to hurt you).

Please forgive me (for whatever I did or did not do).

I love you (unconditionally).

Thank you (for allowing me to right this wrong).

The Ho'oponopono practice might not speak to all of us, but the practice of forgiveness hopefully does. So many of us carry unbearable burdens of emotional baggage, which often has a devastating effect on our lives. It's as if our joy and happiness are being pulled down by emotional wounds that have never been tended to. Forgiving and releasing your emotional baggage is one of the great healings available to everyone, and as you heal yourself, you are healing the world because just like hurt people hurt people, happy people spread happiness.

So be righteously selfish. Forgive and heal yourself. You deserve it.

YOUR TURN

1. What unhealed wounds do you have? (Hint: What triggers you?) What still carries a negative charge? What stops you from moving forward?

2. Separate what actually happened from the story you've created around what happened. The story is the meaning we give something, and the meaning is what holds the negative emotional charge. When you separate the two, you allow yourself space to own what happened and let it go, along with the negative charges.

3. Commit to healing. Commit to wanting to move on. And within that commitment, release the emotional charge by using forgiveness. There are many forgiveness practices. I've highlighted the Ho'oponopono one because it's my favorite, especially as the premise is about taking responsibility, which means taking your power back.

TRANSFORMATION

Everything in life is constantly evolving, changing, and in motion. The dance of life oscillates endlessly between chaos and order, both of which are merely rest stops in our journey. In the depth of chaos rests the seed of order and vice versa.

It's our nature, however, to seek permanence, certainty, and predictability. The mind loathes change and the unknown, so we mindlessly—literally and figuratively—project the past onto the future to create the illusion of certainty. The great irony is that as soon as we learn to accept and embrace uncertainty, we start to live in certainty. We understand that change is the only constant in life, and within that certainty lies our freedom. This is the true paradox of life.

Because we prefer sameness and certainty, we naturally see ourselves, our life, and the world at large as fixed or static. As a result, we have a very limited perspective on what is really possible for us. As we set out into the big grown-up world, we typically start getting "real" about life. Before we know it, we have bills to pay, supposedly defined career paths to walk down, love relationships to move to the next level, and possibly kids to add to the mix because that's what you do next. With some inevitable stumbles and heartbreaks along the way, we soon realize we've gotten on the never enoughitis carousel, spinning and spinning. We know something has gone missing. Our purpose and dreams somehow got lost or watered down in the shuffle, and we don't dare to dream of the life we really want anymore. We become imprisoned in this very narrow view of life.

Before I started awakening, I had a very defined and narrow view of myself. I was an Ivy-league–educated businessman, a real estate developer, an entrepreneur, a husband, a father, and I saw myself as a player in the game of business. However, these were very limiting views of what I was, and they created a very limited space in which I could play.

When I first embarked on my spiritual journey, my self-created box was one of the first things I bumped into. What I was doing and learning was far outside this box I had painted for myself, so it created an inner conflict between the way I had always viewed myself and where my soul was wanting me to go. Letting go of all these old constructs was a big part of breaking free and opening the path to transformation.

Have you put yourself into a narrow box? Could it be this narrow box is limiting your own potential transformation? This chapter will show you how to take responsibility for what you actually control and how to surrender the rest. Transformation is only a decision away.

CHANGE VERSUS TRANSFORMATION

Change and transformation are not the same things; in fact,

they are very different. Change is required for transformation, and all transformation involves change, but not all change is transformation.

Change can be described as a modification of the original state, whereas transformation can be described as a metamorphosis from the original state. Physical objects, or things, can only change; they cannot transform. Human beings have a physical aspect, but we are not things. We are not our form. We are consciousness or awareness itself; we are energetic beings. Energy can transform; therefore, a human being can transform.

Furthermore, transformation of energy, like consciousness, is not bound by time and place as objects in the material world are. Because we are energy, we can transform in an instant—not simply change but transcend your current state to another state in a single moment.

How can you transform? By merely changing your beliefs. With a single decision, you can open up a whole new universe of possibilities. There are infinite possibilities existing in parallel at any moment, and they are all available to you. There is nothing static, fixed, or permanent about you—you are consciousness or awareness—so at any moment, you can transform yourself. You actually get to choose whether to do so.

> "As human beings, our greatness lies not so much in being able to remake the world—that's the myth of the atomic age—as in being able to remake ourselves."
>
> —MAHATMA GANDHI

TRANSFORMATION IS A DECISION AWAY

Have these thoughts triggered a reaction in you? Is something in you resisting the idea that you transform yourself right now if you wanted to?

If so, that's your ego desperately screaming, "No, no, no!" because having the freedom to transform blows up the whole story of self—the story you have about you.

Yes, you are living a story about you. That story is the programming that's running the show, programming that's the invisible hand directing your life until you become aware or experience an awakening. You've built this story over your lifetime. Its building blocks are your upbringing, the cultural and religious values you grew up with, and your experiences, dreams, ideals, romantic notions, fantasies, and stories about what happened and how the world occurs to you. Using these blocks, you have formed an image of yourself, but that image is thought, and thought is not real.

Thoughts (and the brain that produces them) are one and the same, but they are not you. As discussed earlier, you are the consciousness, or awareness, observing your thoughts. Thoughts represent or reflect the past since thought comes from knowledge, and knowledge is past experience stored up in the brain. Thought is, therefore, always limited, just as knowledge is limited.

Since the image you have created about yourself—the self or ego— is thought and thought is not real, the image is nonexistent in terms of being a real, tangible thing. You are thus not defined by this image. You can change this image. You can rewrite this image. In the moment it takes to change a thought, you can transform this image because it is only held together by thought and nothing else.

What does this open up for you? Everything. Your only limitations are the thoughts or beliefs you have about yourself. Does this make you uncomfortable? It should because this puts the responsibility of your life squarely in your hands. Plus, change is uncomfortable, and transformation is change on steroids. Your ego is going to fight you tooth and nail. This kind of transformation is the death of the ego, and the ego doesn't want to die! It's going to do everything in its power to sabotage your efforts to break free from its chains of enslavement. But, ultimately, it's no match for awareness. The ego is like a thick sheet of ice in spring: it will hold on for a long time, but ultimately, it's going to succumb to the piercing rays from the sun, that is, awareness.

When you choose to change your thoughts and transform, you will not only be dueling your ego. You will also be fighting resistance from your family, friends, colleagues, and many others. Your transformation will inspire some but frighten most. As you break free from the chains—the story of your old self—and spread your wings to soar to new heights, your transformation will trigger resentment, envy, jealousy, and even hate from those who aren't there yet. Some of them will ridicule you, try to belittle you, and do everything in their power to prevent you from transforming. People generally want you to stay small, but once these paradigms of awareness shift, you can no longer stay small just for the comfort of others.

Initially, this resistance from the people closest to you might seed doubt and fear of alienation in you, and your ego will clamp on to those emotions to stifle or reverse your progress. But don't let the naysayers deter you. Embrace the resistance with love. It's a signpost that you are on the right path. Remember, transformation is uncomfortable, but as you've learned, discomfort is something to welcome like a trusted old friend. If you're not uncomfortable, you're not growing and becoming the very best version of who you can be.

TAKE RESPONSIBILITY

Our default wiring is to want everything by doing nothing. We want the fit body, but we don't really want to dedicate the time and effort to our workout regimen and diet to get there. We want the nice job and big house, but we don't really want to work hard to get it. Most of us don't really want to sacrifice anything. We're soft—our willpower muscle is weak.

At the core, we don't really want to own or take full responsibility for our lives or our choices. It's much more convenient and comfortable to *not* take a risk, blame things on bad luck, put things off until the "time is right," and so on. We wallow in self-pity and excuses why this or that is not possible or didn't happen, or why we couldn't do it.

Guess what? If you keep doing that, you will be guaranteed the same outcome. Life will be predictable and comfortable, but you won't be growing, changing, or transforming. In so doing, you will almost skillfully avoid the experience of devastating failures, the sour taste of defeat, the utter loneliness of being completely lost, the piercing pain of injury, the unbearable sadness of having your heart broken into a thousand pieces, or the crushing feeling of rejection, loss, or failure. You'll also avoid the soaring joy of truly living. Life will be safe, but it will also be gray and muted. And you will blend right in, too, because this is how most people choose to live life.

You can run out the days of your life on autopilot, letting your ego take control and run the programming. Or you can take full responsibility for your reality and every aspect of your life.

Taking responsibility is the only answer when you say, "Fuck this mediocre life bullshit," and are no longer willing to color within the lines defined by the *brules* of your upbringing, culture, religious dogma, or society as a whole. In taking responsibility, you insist on defining your own lines to color within. You make life into your own masterpiece.

If anything less than the very best version of yourself is simply no longer an option, you're ready to take responsibility. You are willing to accept and fully embrace the downside because you insist on experiencing epic wins, the sweet taste of victory, the peace of finding your path, the deep bliss of good health, the immeasurable natural high of being totally lost in love, and the illuminating glory of acceptance, gain, or success. You know there will be challenges and obstacles, but that's okay. You're ready for whatever shows up.

The moment you fully accept you are not fixed, you bust the door to transformation wide open. You can reprogram the programs no longer serving you and replace them with programs and beliefs that do. You can heal old wounds, learn from the past, and reinvent yourself in any which way you choose. You still have to do the work, but embracing change is possible, and taking responsibility for whatever happens is the crucial first step.

Knowing is powerful, but without right action in response, it's meaningless. Reading the *Kama Sutra* is not going to make you a great lover. You have to get into the arena and bring your knowledge into practice through right action.

What is right action? It's bringing those thoughts and beliefs that serve you and your purpose into action. Actions contrary to or inconsistent with those thoughts and beliefs are self-sabotaging and counterproductive. You know whether certain actions serve you or not, but bringing right action into reality isn't always easy or natural. For example, people know smoking is wrong, but they still have a hard time quitting. Likewise, people know they should eat healthy, but their compulsion to eat junk food might be stronger than that knowledge. This is self-sabotage.

To choose right action, you have to give yourself permission to change, evolve, and transform. Nobody else can do this for you. You have to create the space for the new and transformed version of yourself. Self-sabotage shows up because giving yourself permission is a mighty threshold to cross. As you seek to step across that threshold, historical baggage—your upbringing, cultural or religious dogmas, and societal norms—will be holding you back like chains anchored in cement. Giving yourself permission to transform allows you to break free from those chains, but as we've said, your ego doesn't want this. Transformation is the death of the old, in this case, your old thoughts and beliefs, and your ego is going to put up a fight. Rebirth is a messy and sometimes violent process—before something new can be born, something else has to die.

Are you allowing yourself to become a much grander version of you? Have you given yourself permission to become the very best you can be, no matter what anybody says or does? Ask yourself these questions often. The answers will reveal the extent to which you are giving yourself permission to transform.

The good news is that we only have to take responsibility for the piece of the pie that we actually control. In the big scheme of things, that piece is infinitesimally small. It appears and often feels huge, but figuratively speaking, it's tiny—less than a drop in the ocean.

We also don't have to concern ourselves with time travel with this practice because we cannot affect anything in the past or the future. What we are responsible for—our right action—can only be done in the present moment.

You are responsible for right action, right now, and that's it. Nothing else. The rest we leave in the capable hands of the universe, God, Infinite Intelligence, source, or whatever you want to call the higher power. Relinquishing the rest is called "surrendering."

SURRENDER

Most of us, myself included, are hardwired to believe that, through effort or force, we can shape our world and create our reality. To some extent, that's true: our effort (or lack thereof) seemingly makes a vast difference in what we accomplish or fail to accomplish. But that's not the whole story.

For anything to show up in your life, an infinite number of factors beyond your personal efforts had to line up perfectly. It's delusional to think we control all of those variables to make our circumstances what they are.

That means either random luck or some intelligence far greater than our own is at play here. I have seen enough evidence to know it's all directed in intelligent ways by an intelligence far greater than our own, but it actually doesn't matter if these infinite variables are controlled by luck or a higher being. The bottom line is you don't control them, and you never will. You can fear them, curse them, try to manipulate or bend them, but it's futile in the end. Rather than fight them, accept that you control very little, take full responsibility for right action where you can, and surrender to the benevolent universe for the rest. Surrender like this is a daily spiritual practice.

Surrender is an act of faith, complete trust or confidence in someone or something, even when you cannot see, validate, or prove its existence. How do you have faith in a higher power you cannot adequately describe in words, let alone unequivocally prove to exist? That's why it's called faith. We don't have proof of this higher power, at least not tangible proof in this dense material world. But this higher power is not from our material world, so to seek evidence within this realm is like looking for the desert in the ocean.

What we can do is go within. When we go within, beyond our own form and thought, we encounter the stillness that is our awareness. Through awareness, we are all connected to this higher power, Infinite Intelligence, God, and benevolent universe—whatever name you choose.

Meditation, breathwork, and certain forms of yoga are just some of the tools we can use to quiet the mind and access awareness. As we do, our body shifts to the parasympathetic nervous system ("rest and relax"), which has a calming effect on our entire physiology and allows it to move into repair and regeneration mode. Cultivating a relationship with this stillness helps slow life down from the daily treadmill we're on, and within that stillness, we have access to clarity, calm, peace, and a sense of appreciation for the vastness of the universe and the intelligence and beauty in all of it. Faith that there is a larger intelligence at work and that things don't happen randomly starts to organically build within when we make it a daily practice to slow down our thoughts—in whatever way works for us—and access this stillness of our awareness.

How do you develop faith you can feel? Start attributing everything good that has ever happened to you that you cannot explain solely based on your own efforts and action to this higher power or intelligence. That job you won out because their first choice accepted another position, the imminent car accident you narrowly avoided, the love of your life you met at a place you never go—the list is endless. Your whole life is one giant soup of seemingly serendipitous events and occurrences, and you have very little to do with any of it. You still have to show up for life and do your part, but deep down, we all know that most of life just shows up. It just happens, miraculously.

Once you see the miraculous nature of your life, faith becomes something you feel. That's the moment faith penetrates your soul, and you can't help but trust in the infinitely intelligent ways of the universe and how life is always working for you. What more proof do you need? Just look around. Examine the events that make up your life. Once you accept your own limited role, faith gives you freedom. Freedom from fear, freedom from doubt, and the freedom to play all out within this reality we call life.

With faith on your side and the winds of the benevolent universe in your sails, you are free to be whatever you want to be. You are free to grow, evolve, change, and transform at any moment. You are not whatever image you have of yourself in the past. Right here, right now, you are free to step into the new you. Transformation is your birthright, and you have full permission to change, to grow, to evolve, and to transform.

Faith and trusting the universe will have your back will be the winds beneath your wings. Maybe you cannot see the wind, but you will feel it once you jump off the cliff and allow yourself the freedom to transform.

YOUR TURN

1. Describe how you see yourself. Write down all the things you "are," which might include your profession (e.g., lawyer, doctor, yoga instructor), a role (e.g., mother, father, friend, etc.), characteristics (e.g., adventurous, smart, shy), or something you associate with (e.g., American, environmentalist, sailor, etc.). You may have written a similar list for the first question in the "You" chapter. See if you can add to it.

2. Look at your list and ask yourself, "Is this all that I am?" All these descriptors are actually just thoughts or labels you use to define yourself. Since these things define you, they also limit you.

3. What's not on this list that you feel you are or want to be? How is this list limiting you in how you can show up? Who or what would you "be" in your dream life? Why is that not possible?

LOVE

The essence of love is as easy to distill into words as it is to capture the ocean in a bathtub. Love is so vast and has so many facets and nuances. I've come to believe that at its very core, love is the energy or universal life force (or Chi, or Prana, or Shakti) that originated, animates, and weaves through all creation. Since the universal life force is divine consciousness, love—the energy, not the emotion—is pure consciousness.

Love, the emotion, is a singular feeling of affection you might feel for a person, an animal, or even a hobby or profession. This kind of love can be felt toward ourselves and others in a platonic or romantic way.

Love the energy, however, refers to a state of being. In Christianity, this state of being is also referred to as our Christ nature, and in Buddhism, it's referred to as our Buddha nature. In both instances, love, the energy, refers to a state of elevated consciousness—an awakened state—where we start to fully embody the energy of love in all that we say, do, and project into the world. It's this energy and compassion that our world needs a lot more of if we are to chart a different course and create a new earth, but more on that later.

In this chapter, we'll look at some of the facets of love and the need for self-love to fully realize any of the other nuances. We'll also touch on the interplay between masculine and feminine energies and the result in the world we see today.

SELF-LOVE AND ONENESS

There are many variants of love—unconditional, affectionate, romantic, familiar, universal—but as long as the egoic mind is the director of your life, for the most part, you're living in the illusion of love. The egoic mind creates your identity of self, which is by nature separate from the rest of the world and is the essence of duality. We cannot truly love until we embrace the concept of oneness, and the path to oneness is self-love.

Why oneness? Until we see and feel how we're all connected, related, and exist as a very small part of the whole, it's quite challenging to see ourselves, or anyone else for that matter, as already whole and complete. We're always judging and comparing ourselves to others when there's really nothing to compare. We're all one-of-a-kind, totally unique expressions of Infinite Intelligence. A beautiful tree doesn't compare itself to the next tree, and a dolphin doesn't compare its jumps with the dolphin jumping alongside it, and in similar fashion, we shouldn't compare ourselves with others.

In the process of embodying self-love, you will find that the principle of oneness grows from an awareness to an undeniable truth.

Your view of the world and everything in it will evolve. The fact that everything is connected and is a divine expression of Infinite Intelligence will become self-evident, and your experience of the pain, hardships, and suffering of mankind, animals, and Mother Earth will likely change radically. That's because you're leaving a place of unconsciousness in the mind and moving to a state of higher consciousness in the heart—love. From a place of fullness, of being complete and whole, love and compassion become a state of being. You are no longer guided or held hostage by the lower frequency of fear, and with this raised frequency, life shifts dramatically for you. Love and relationships become deeper, richer, and more vibrant, as they are no longer based on needing anything in return.

Until we are whole and complete, until we embrace oneness, being our authentic self and living our truth in a state of self-love, we're in the business of what I like to call "transactional love."

In a state of self-love, you don't need anything. You are already complete. You are free to give without ever running out because, in this state, love is an abundant bottomless well that originates from within. In the absence of self-love, love is merely a currency that you trade for reciprocal love, validation, admiration, favor, being liked, security, fitting in, filling a void, or whatever else your ego hungers for or your soul might be lacking. It might look and feel like genuine love to you, but as long you *need* love to be whole, it's not love. It's a business deal.

This doesn't mean we don't set healthy boundaries or gracefully withdraw ourselves from those relationships that aren't serving us. It also doesn't mean we never get hurt or that we're immune to heartbreak. Of course, we're still human. We're going to feel shit until the day we die. But when we come from a place of self-love, we deal with the hurt or heartbreak in constructive ways. We nurse our wounds, grieve our losses, and take care of our scars, so we heal and move on, but we don't ever doubt that we're good enough or that we deserve friendship or love in our life, or that we are worthy because, coming from a place of self-love, we know we are.

In keeping with the laws of the universe, Infinite Intelligence always acts in intelligent ways, so intelligence loves itself unconditionally. Anything else would be unintelligent. When you return to self-love (yes, return, for self-love is our natural state as young children until we develop an ego), you're returning to your natural state of intelligence, which is a state of abundance of love for everyone and everything—including yourself. The Bible states, "My cup runneth over" (Psalm 23:5), which means "I have more than enough for my needs." Only when you're whole and complete, being your authentic self in a state of self-love, will your cup overflow. In the not-needing, you can give freely for the sake of giving—and that is real, unconditional love.

UNCONDITIONAL LOVE

In good times, unconditional love is as easy as sailing downwind on a breezy day. The true test if you have embodied this love is when shit doesn't go the way you planned or want it to go—when someone hurts your feelings, when someone steals from you, when the inevitable injustices of life knock on your door, when the world seems such an unfair place, and when your heart gets broken in ten thousand pieces. Even the most evolved among us has days when it seems much easier to blame than love. But that's not unconditional love. The very name indicates that no matter what happens, you will still love the other person. You will see through what happened and accept total responsibility—because it showed up in your life, you take responsibility for creating it.

When I got divorced in late 2017, after nearly fourteen years of marriage, I went through a whirlwind of emotions. I was a hot mess with a bleeding heart, even though I had initiated the divorce. When Cara began dating shortly after we separated, I don't know which was scarred more, my ego or my heart.

One night, I was overcome with sadness, and wallowing in self-pity, I called a dear friend, who shifted my experience once and for all by asking a few simple questions:

"Do you love her? Not romantically, but do you love her for the person that she is?" my friend asked.

"Of course, I do," I answered.

"If that's true, wouldn't you want her to be happy?"

"Yes, I guess so."

"If that is so, who are you crying for?"

A big silence followed on my side. In that moment, my friend helped me realize I was acting out of a lack of self-love—I wasn't whole and complete in myself, so I needed Cara to miss me. My ego was directing the show. I was operating from old patterns and not living from the heart. In that moment, I wasn't whole and complete, and for that reason, I had no capacity to love Cara unconditionally—to let her find her happiness and do what was best for her to heal her broken heart.

My friend continued. "If you truly, unconditionally love someone, you continue to do so even when the form changes."

The next day, I started intensive therapy, which was my tenuous first step to finding self-love and truly living from the heart.

Unconditional love is pure life force—it's uplifting, empowering, nurturing, healing, and forgiving, and it can only come from a place of self-love when your cup is overflowing. If you want to get to know and experience true love, including unconditional love, self-love is always the place to start.

ROMANTIC LOVE

Romantic love, with her army of oxytocin soldiers, she's the most potent love force known to mankind—pure, unadulterated magic. (If you don't know what I'm talking about, put this book down immediately and go live life! Find love!)

Romantic love makes us blind. In fact, we're chemically wired that way.[5] When you're falling head over heels, oxytocin (the love hormone) and dopamine (the pleasure hormone) are secreted in copious amounts by the pituitary gland, flooding your brain and bloodstream with an intoxicating cocktail that also includes adrenaline and norepinephrine. It actually shuts down certain

---

5   Theresa L. Crenshaw, *The Alchemy of Love and Lust* (New York: Pocket Books, 1996).

parts of your brain that have to do with visual discernment. This is nature's way of making sure the person looks like the handsome prince or gorgeous princess you want to see.

As these hormones race through your body, all discernment goes out the door, leaving you under the wonderful spell of lust, attraction, and attachment, driven by intense desire. There's no drug that will ever get you as high as romantic love. This is the essence of not just life but being alive.

However, so many of us have gotten our hearts broken at some point, or maybe many points, and each time this happens, we close off a little more. We never quite dare to go all in again. We guard our mushy hearts because the scars never quite heal. It takes much bravery to be vulnerable again, to open our hearts fully and trust. Yet vulnerability is where all the ecstasy and magic are. We forget that when we're heartbroken, we are hardly broken—we are on the path as we're supposed to be. Everything happens for us, even heartbreak. It's good to take time to heal and reflect, but to not venture back into the arena, or to do so half-heartedly, is to rob yourself of the potential magic. Even more so, it's selfish because you're robbing someone else of the magic they could have with you.

Admittedly, I am a complete romantic fool. I love hard, and I hurt hard, and my heart has been broken more times than I care to admit. But after some time passes, I have always found ways to grow from the relationship that wasn't meant to be, to learn lessons, and most importantly, to get a better idea of what my dream goddess is like in every way. I've come to embrace the idea that I am one step closer to finding her each time a relationship ends.

By now, my desired list of attributes and qualities is so long and detailed that I don't waste a lot of time on goddesses I know aren't a good fit. Why should either of us invest our time and hearts into something that's not going to go anywhere meaningful? My discernment has gone way up, and my mindless dating has gone way down. In fact, I really don't date much at all anymore. However, when I meet someone who captures my undivided interest and imagination, I act immediately because life is fleeting. She will know my interest quickly, as I will shower her with my every iota of charm and thoughtfulness. There's no point in leaving her in the dark about how I feel.

Yes, I will feel vulnerable as fuck in that moment, but at the same time, I am buzzing with excitement. I don't worry or think about rejection because what you think is what you attract. I only think about the magic that could be. I live in the potential of it all. I enjoy the dreamy dance, and I surrender to the fact that I have nothing to say about the outcome; that's in the stars.

Even if you have scars or fear rejection, please don't ever lose your foolish romantic ways. Love is the most high.

> "Every heart sings a song, incomplete, until another heart whispers back. Those who dare to sing always find a song."
>
> —PLATO

Of course, romantic love is much more than that euphoric bliss trip that is so aptly called the "honeymoon period." When the hormone cocktail wears off, we sail into the attachment phase, where we deepen our connection, sense of well-being, and security within the relationship. Esther Perel, in her ground-breaking book *Mating in Captivity*, brought many relationships myths, dynamics, and pitfalls to light. She highlights how, in the attachment phase, the killers of relationships can slowly creep in, mostly familiarity and dullness.

With two divorces under my belt, I am no relationship expert—or maybe I am. But after reading Perel's book, I started recognizing the truth of the dynamics she writes and speaks about, and I have become an avid student of her work. Most of us believe we're natural-born lovers and perfect partners—men especially. The truth is, most of us have no clue, and until we decide to learn and grow and become better at relationships—understanding the sacred dance between the masculine and feminine, love, and even making love—we're just stuck in low gear and are missing out on what's possible.

I know now that I was absolutely clueless about what I wanted or needed, let alone how to create it. I had no North Star whatsoever, so I was just winging it (clearly, two divorces later). Over the last few years, as I started to examine what's important for me, I decided I needed a North Star. I needed to crystallize what's truly important so I could begin to seek and create that in my life.

For me, that North Star comes down to the realization of four core desires: deep love, deep connection, deep commitment, and crazy good lovemaking. Those might not be your top four. You might have totally different needs and desires, and your list might have nine things instead of four. Whatever it is for you, be clear about it, and let that guide you in all you do toward creating and manifesting that magical romantic relationship into your life.

For me to be in the epic relationship I want, with all four desires present, I have to show up and do my part. I can't expect deep love if I show up with a closed-off heart; if I neglect her feelings, wishes, and desires; or if I show up in any way that's inconsistent with deep love. I also crave a deep connection, and to have that, I have to open up and let her in, no matter if that sometimes scares the piss out of me because of some old wounds. If I want that deep connection, I need to make her feel connected to me first.

I still believe in fairy tales and happily (forever) after. For that to happen, I need to be faithful, truthful, trustworthy, and act with integrity. She will never trust me without those things, and without trust, we will never have that connection or commitment or longevity I long for.

The last one, crazy good lovemaking, is more than the law of reciprocity that says unless I am the best lover she has ever had, she won't ever become mine. There's much more to crazy good lovemaking than that. When you make love, you connect deeply on a physical level, but it can also foster a deep spiritual connection. This is the essence of the *Kama Sutra* teachings. The old sages knew that through the sacred art—not *act*—of lovemaking, you can reach and create a deep spiritual connection well beyond the physical. There's another bonus: the love hormone oxytocin is released during lovemaking, which turns every great love session into a mini excursion back to the original bliss of the honeymoon period. This is why so many relationship experts emphasize the importance of intimacy in a love relationship because these moments of shared ecstasy are what make us feel deeply connected—and lack of intimacy makes us feel more disconnected.

The art of making sex "crazy good" is to keep it novel, spicy, kinky even, to reinvent and get creative, to try new things, share and act out fantasies, and keep an element of surprise and novelty. All of that requires being vulnerable and open, and in all your nakedness (literal and figurative), completely surrendering to the moment. This is where creating a safe place for radical honesty is a beautiful way to deepen the sharing and connection. If you commit to traveling to that RH space together, this deep level of intimacy is the ultimate fortifier of trust and the sacred bond between lovers. This is where you can, not merely as lovers but as soul mates, go on this deep, spiritual journey together, peeling away the many masks we wear and old wounds we carry, so we strip down to our true essence, our authentic self.

This sort of lovemaking, the merging of the sacred masculine and divine feminine energies, is of a cosmic nature, and the healing powers of love, of life force, will reverberate into every corner of your being. This is where the whole universe comes to a momentary standstill, stars collide, and there's an orgasmic explosion of love so powerful you know you have been touched by the divine. You can only journey there together, and this is where the true magic is.

Esther Perel articulates so eloquently that we have seemingly diametrically opposed needs of *security*, which comes from familiarity, and *novelty*, which comes from adventure. Everything known is familiar and, therefore, safe; everything new is adventure and, therefore, novel. The unknown is uncomfortable, but that's where the sassy edge of excitement lives. Crazy good lovemaking, then, is pure relationship building. It invites and spills over into all the other vital parts of your relationship, and I can't imagine a more wonderful way to make things better and better.

UNIVERSAL LOVE

If love, at its core, is consciousness, then what is the opposite? In an emotional sense, the opposite of love might be hate, apathy, or indifference, but on the ethereal energy dimension, the opposite of love cannot be anything but unconsciousness.

When I look around at the world humans have created, I see a man-made world—that is, a world made from masculine energy—created from the mind and not the heart. Wars, famine, hunger, racial and religious divides, extreme concentration of wealth, widespread abuse of women and children, rampant pollution of our oceans and waterways, widespread deforestation, loss of wildlife and eradication of animal species in staggering numbers, the slaughter of 150 billion animals a year, chemtrails, fracking, 5G, genetically modified food devoid of any nutritional value, a populace that's, on average, malnourished or grossly overweight and uses more pharmaceuticals, drugs, and alcohol than at any time in history—this world could only have been created with a collective level of unconsciousness that's deeply rooted in fear.

These acts of self-interest or greed stem from fear. Fear of not being enough, fear of not having enough, fear of lack, fear of scarcity—the list goes on. This same fear is at the root of never enoughitis. No matter how hard we strive, how much money we make, how many toys we buy, it's never fucking enough, but we continue accumulating more and more, despite the unintelligence in all of it. The wars, famine, divides, inequalities, injustices, pollution, and destruction of the very planet that gives us life are all highly unintelligent acts resulting from fear. Our way of being and living are highly unintelligent. Humanity's actions are downright stupid, actually, because we are literally exterminating ourselves in rapid fashion.

What is the answer? How do we fix this troubled world? How do we stop acting out of fear and self-interest? We return to universal love by raising our collective consciousness.

For centuries, we have rendered the feminine energy a second-class citizen in the creation of our world, and until we restore the divine feminine energy to its rightful place alongside and in full emancipation with the masculine, we are going to get more of the same. In other words, we need to start living from the heart instead of the mind. A world created intelligently by consciousness with universal love from the heart simply would not look like the one in which we live. A world created in intelligent ways through universal love would be heaven on earth.

To move in this direction, action is needed by both men and women. Men tend to be masculine energy dominant, acting from the mind, and women feminine energy dominant, acting from the heart, but we all have elements of both. To raise our collective consciousness, the masculine needs to restore the mind-heart connection that has been lying dormant for so long and rediscover, cultivate, and embrace the feminine within. Creating this world will not happen from force, power, greed, and relentless doing. The human species can no longer rationalize its way out of the atrocities and violence we justify under the disguise of economic necessity. We have to restore balance and harmony on all levels.

At the same time, the feminine has to step into its power, not by vilifying the masculine but by embodying their divine feminine significance as self-evident simply by being. As long as the feminine seeks its significance to be granted and recognized by the masculine, it is giving away its true power by placing itself in a position of needing validation from the masculine. (In my opinion, this has been the weak link all along in the modern feminist movement that had its origins in the 1960s.) The moment the feminine simply is, and needs no validation or recognition from the masculine (or anything external for that matter), it has claimed sovereignty.

I believe we are already heading in this direction, as an energy shift has begun. Mother Earth, Gaia, is a living, breathing entity that has its own frequency, and she has awakened from a long slumber to ring in a new era. The COVID-19 pandemic coincided with a seismic shift in the energy balance, and we are moving from a masculine energy–dominant world to a feminine energy–dominant world.[6]

Women will naturally rise and blossom in this environment, as their feminine energy dominance will be a vibrational match with the new frequency of Mother Earth and the shifting sands of the universe. Old structures and paradigms will start to crumble as this new world slowly emerges from the fog of transition that we're in right now.

Change comes with chaos and disruption, but within it is the seed of opportunity for humanity to create a new earth and abort the disastrous trajectory we have been on. This shift is not a problem

---

6   For more on this idea, see Christina Lopes's YouTube channel, *The Heart Alchemist*, as well as her website at Christina-Lopes.com.

for men unless we stubbornly hold on to the old ways. In fact, it's a call to action for men to evolve, grow, and awaken.

Our economy and unbridled consumerism will inevitably shift from a cradle-to-grave philosophy to a cradle-to-cradle philosophy[7] so that we can effectively counter the depleting availability of natural resources in tandem with the rising global population. We have to embrace and speed up green energy so we can wean off our dependence on fossil fuel-derived power. We already have the technologies to do so. Covering a mere 3 percent of the earth's surface with solar panels can power the entire world,[8] and electric vehicles have long been technologically superior to their combustion engine equivalents. These changes will create epic economic opportunities, so there are zero arguments to be made that these shifts will diminish the abundance available to any of us.[9] On a societal level, the innate ability of the feminine to unite and harmonize will create the fertile soil for real change to address such deep-rooted schisms as racism, hate, and inequality.

If we don't realize these beautiful changes and instead stubbornly maintain business as usual, we will continue on the bullet train to disaster. Unless we radically alter the way we live, our children will not be able to see live coral, breathe clean air, enjoy abundant wildlife, or live in low-lying places likely to be swallowed whole by rising sea levels. This isn't about creating some sort of woo-woo Utopian society. This is about survival of the species, and it's

---

7   *Cradle to Cradle: Remaking the Way We Make Things* (New York: North Point Press, 2002) by Michael Braungart and William McDonough is a must read if this topic has your interest.

8   Land Art Generator, www.landartgenerator.org/infographics.html.

9   This new form of capitalism—often referred to as conscious capitalism—has the potential to lift all ships and right the many excesses and wrongs that have crept into the system through various forms of crony capitalism.

a mere few minutes to midnight! We must start to embody and create from a place of universal love, approaching people, nature, animals, and all things from a place of compassion and respect. We must commit to making intelligent decisions that ensure that everyone can thrive, including Mother Earth.

This journey is one of raising our collective frequency so that we all rise to ever-higher levels of consciousness, and in that journey, we start to embody universal love, celebrate and fuse the masculine and feminine energies, and that's how we create a new earth.

LIVE AND LOVE

As we approach the end of this book, it's hopefully clear by now that I believe in manifestation and that we are the creators of our own reality. One of the biggest challenges in this journey called life is the sense of separation between what we want and what we currently have. If the thing we want is not right here, right now, it's often just not real to us.

Consider this. I know my dream goddess is out there, and I know deep down in my heart that I will meet her at the perfect time. The fact I haven't met her yet doesn't mean she doesn't exist. She's right there, in potentiality, in all her absolute perfection as perceived through my lens. I am not separated at all from what I want, for I have zero doubt that she is real. My only task right now, until I meet her, is to become the man she would fall in love with.

Go live life. Live it in love—with yourself foremost and, if you so desire, with your other. But definitely live it in love with the whole world around you.

YOUR TURN

1. Are you kind and loving to yourself? Do you judge yourself? Do you live in self-love or self-loathing? Try seeing yourself as you would a five-year-old. Would you tell your five-year-old self that you're too fat or that you have an ugly nose? Remember this the next time you speak harshly to yourself.

2. Do you love for the sake of loving, or do you seek recognition for your loving acts? How often do you express love through anonymous acts? Practice unconditional love by loving for the sake of being kind and expecting nothing in return.

3. In your most intimate relationships with family, friends, and/or your lover, be the one to unconditionally give first. This is challenging because we get hurt and easily offended. Our hearts are mushy, and going first makes us feel vulnerable. Do it anyway; you harvest what you seed.

JUST LOVE HER

Over the past five years, as I've pursued my spiritual journey, delving ever deeper into the many complex layers that make up each of us, I was often faced with unforgiving and painful truths. Personal mastery pursued in earnest involves looking into the dark corners of your being. This spiritual cleansing process is ruthless, and I commend all who are on the path themselves.

One of the darkest shadows for me has been my relationship to and with women. The many personal development and spiritual retreats I've participated in have provided the most confronting of mirrors. These workshops tend to be predominantly attended by women, which means I typically found myself to be one of the few men attending in a sea of women.

Many of these retreats create a container or safe place so that as the spiritual deep dive commences, they can crack you wide open. In those spaces, many courageous and strong spiritual warrior goddesses shared their deep wounds, and many of those wounds involved rape, molestation, physical and emotional abuse, abandonment, and more. In most cases, these disgusting violations had come from males they trusted, whether it was their father, sibling, uncle, boyfriend, or husband. They revealed deep emotional scars from these experiences that prevented them from trusting, loving, and opening up their hearts to any man.

Although I have never violated a woman in any of those atrocious ways, I was confronted with how I had objectified women in general, how I had been a womanizer since my teens, pursuing, courting, seducing, and charming ladies without ever pausing to consider the hearts I might have broken, simply because I had the urge to play the game.

As I've mentioned, I'm also a romantic fool and am entirely guilty of adoring women. As I witnessed firsthand the deep wounds caused by men like me, followed by an internal recognition of how I had been showing up in life, my heart finally broke into a thousand pieces, and I was forced to own my past and transform my relationship to and with women.

The final straw was a retreat I attended in 2017 in Mexico, where it came to my awareness by witnessing the stories of the women there, as obvious as it sounds, that each of the women I had ever seduced or objectified had been someone's daughter. It made me think of my own effervescent love for my little girl, seven at the time, who was innocence embodied. That realization crushed me. I love my little girl more than life itself. She's my angel, my princess, the love of my life. In that moment, something inside me shifted, and I've never looked at women in the same way since.

Along with this shift came a long-overdue recognition of the inherent value and beauty of the divine feminine. Before that retreat, I didn't really understand what feminine energy was, let alone the vastness of its grace and strength, or how the masculine and feminine are designed to be opposites and complements at the same time.

With this newfound perspective, I embarked on a journey to study and learn more about feminine energy and all it entails. This led me to read visionary books, such as *The Way of the Superior Man* by David Deida and many others.

All the beauty, intelligence value, creation, passion, love, and grace this world has to offer is captured in the divine feminine. Our human goddesses are the embodiment of this divine energy. To restore that masculine-feminine balance and embrace the universal love that will pave the way for a new world, we men need to embrace the feminine by valuing, respecting, and loving our human goddesses.

In one way or another, we all have women in our lives, but the most powerful teacher will always be your own goddess if you're lucky enough to have one grace your life. We learn through osmosis by respecting, recognizing, and acknowledging the feminine in the goddess(es) in our lives, for all its worth, majesty, and magnificence. We learn by seeing the valuable qualities our goddess embodies and the grace of her ways. We learn by acknowledging her incredible resilience and strength, even when it's dressed up in a display of feelings and emotions that we men have traditionally equated with weakness. We learn by recognizing the value of her intuitive wisdom and her ability to unite and harmonize, though our natural instincts are to compete and seek dominance. We learn by seeking to become better men.

We have to shift our relationship with the feminine. It's time to grow up. Men, we have a wound to heal. Over millennia, we have suppressed the feminine within us, and until we heal these wounds, we're all just boys in a man's body.

This has nothing to do with men becoming feminine. We simply need to learn to value and love the feminine for what she represents. It's the yin-yang energy balance coming full circle.

To embrace the divine feminine, we need to just love her.

We, the masculine, may have been granted dominion of the world, but we must never forget that the feminine governs the universe. The feminine is the creator of life. Her body, whether your goddess or Mother Earth, is not an inanimate object created for your lust, pleasure, and exploitation. It's the sacred temple that creates all life, so treat it accordingly. Respect the feminine and all her mysterious ways, which oftentimes make no sense to your masculine mind. The fact you won't always be able to grasp her essence takes nothing away from its validity. The truth is you're not supposed to. Just love her.

Just like in the animal kingdom, your masculine architecture is one of action, single-minded focus, purpose, decisiveness, protecting, consciousness, and logic, and linear thinking. You are ruled by the mind and fueled by challenge. The feminine energy embodied by your goddess is one of pure and unbridled life-giving creation, passion, emotion, unpredictability, and intuitive and nonlinear thinking. She lives from the heart and responds to love and praise.

The masculine and feminine are perfect complements, equal

in every respect, but at the same time, opposites by design. The very polarity of the two creates the opportunity to become whole by merging. The feminine is not like you, and she never will be. When you find her difficult, unreasonable, or challenging, just know she's only testing your love for her. Never turn your back. Lean in instead and fearlessly open your heart and let her feel your love. She's not receptive to any of your words of logic or reason. Just love her.

Enjoying her love and divine body is like being immersed in sweet nectar. Nothing compares, and nothing will illuminate your masculine essence as much as the love of your goddess. However, the feminine cannot give herself and love you in the way that moves mountains, parts oceans, and opens skies unless she can trust you.

Your job is to create trust, to be a steadfast rock of unshakable commitment with a fearless, open heart so the feminine can let her untampered, passionate, creative force of life and love flow through her freely. Even when her sometimes unpredictable ways test the limits of your logical mind, guard the trust like your most coveted possession by staying present with an open heart, even when it hurts. The hurt will only be temporary. Her radiant love in exchange is eternal. Just love her.

Whatever the feminine says will always be the truest expression of her feelings in that very moment. Let go of the idea that her words should pass your test of reason to be valid. Her words are merely a reflection of her feelings in the now. Your track record has no credence in the now. Scorecards don't count, and you get no points for past good behavior or future promises. Let go of all of that.

Most likely, her true grievance is she isn't feeling your love. These are warning signs that you have eroded the trust, and the flame of your love has diminished in magnitude, so you have taken away the fuel to her fire. Flare up your flame, make her feel your love in the far corners of her heart, and like clouds in the sky being moved by the prevailing winds, her expressions will shift toward you. All of this is just a dance between the sacred masculine and divine feminine. Just love her.

The very essence of masculinity, the way of the Sacred King, is to live a life of integrity. Always be faithful, truthful, trustworthy, and impeccable with your words. The wounds you impart on your goddess's heart by not living these virtues might very well never heal. You will dim her flame and rob her of her divine radiance, and in turn, you will never be the man you could be, as only in the luminosity of her full radiance can you become the highest version of yourself. Your power to leave a mark on this world rests within her love for you.

For her, for you, for all of mankind, just love her.

YOUR TURN

1. What's your relationship with the feminine? Do you objectify women? Do you downplay the inherent value of her qualities or see them as inferior to the masculine traits of single-minded focus, decisiveness, logic, and linear thinking?

2. What do you view as the cause of the myriad of problems the world has today: wars, violence, hate, racism, famine, inequality, pollution, climate change, deforestation, loss of wildlife? Do you rationalize these things away as the inevitable by-product of our economic progress, or are you hungry for change fueled by compassion and a desire for more unity, harmony, and balance?

3. Can you see how the imbalance between the masculine and feminine has created the world we live in today? All change starts within. How can you restore more balance with yourself between these two energies?

CONCLUSION

As I write this, we are in the midst of the COVID-19 pandemic. Our country is in varying degrees of lockdown, and the economy is struggling. This crisis has laid bare how our collective vision of success has hollowed out the very fabric of society—the ideas and principles that were so eloquently captured by the founding fathers in our Declaration of Independence.

Ten years from now, I believe we will look back at this moment as a turning point. Many structures, corporate and otherwise, will come tumbling down, and we will be forced to reinvent ourselves. The way we have been doing things is simply not sustainable. I should know. I've been there.

I pursued worldly success with gusto. I swam with the sharks until I became one of them. I ended up being a custom-made suit-wearing success in the eyes of the world, but I had lost all touch with what really matters in life. I journeyed into the dark void of greed, corruption, excess, indulgence, selfishness, power games, abuse of leverage, and self-dealing, all in the name of success, and it took me many years to finally see the illusion in it all.

My awakening was forced upon me by my own circumstances

almost five years ago. I have no doubt many others will find themselves in a similar situation when the economic hangover from this crisis wipes out lifetimes of dreams and hard work.

You might be one of those people. Or maybe life will happen for you in another way: a marriage that's lost its passion, a serious illness, the death of a loved one, or some other display of chaos. In some way, life might bring you to a place where you start to question everything you thought to be true, everything you thought would make you happy and fulfilled. Someday, you might be brought face-to-face with your form of never enoughitis, just like I was.

When that happens, the truths you thought were real, your entire reality, will have the look of a deflated balloon that gets trampled when the party is over. You will want to go back to normal only to find normal doesn't exist anymore. What will you do?

My hope is that you embark on a journey within. My hope is that you learn from my lows and see that transformation is within your reach, just as it was for me. You have the power within to heal and reinvent yourself. You have masculine and feminine energy, which, when brought into balance and harmony, can become a powerful healing force in your life and the many lives you touch.

When we each change ourselves—when we find that eternal flame of peace, satisfaction, and fulfillment within—we're not simply changing ourselves. We are changing the world. Each person is a small piece of energy connected to the whole universe. If one piece of energy moves or changes, it affects every other piece. You can only transform your little piece of energy, but your piece is magnificent and powerful and impactful.

The way you show up affects this world—from a conversation with your closest loved ones to your kind word to the person at the take-out counter to the person halfway around the world who reads one of your Instagram posts and draws inspiration. The ripple effects of everything you do are enormous.

As Gandhi said, "Be the change you want to see in the world."

Be radically honest. Be vulnerable. Love with all you've got. As you step into the arena and take responsibility for your life, watch the ripples make their positive impact on the world around you.

All the things you deeply long for—meaning, purpose, joy, happiness, fulfillment, abundance—originate from within. You will not find these things in your career or money or success. You won't even find it in relationships. These things are simply a means to an end. We can derive joy, happiness, and even inspiration from these means, but true, lasting happiness and fulfillment is an inside job. To get to the gold that's buried deep within, you have to take a sometimes soul-wrenching, typically uncomfortable, occasionally terrifying, but ultimately liberating journey within.

Life has a way of taking you where you need to go at the perfect time and place. My wish for you is that you take the plunge because I know the magic you will find when you do.

I see you, and the view is magnificent.

Love and truth,
Robert

ABOUT THE AUTHOR

ROBERT ALTHUIS is the Founder of The Whisperer, a mindfulness organization that provides coaching, strategies, tools, and techniques to help private clients and businesses find their "why" so they can become a force of good in the world. He was once an Ivy League-educated Fortune 100 corporate executive and later a successful real estate and private equity entrepreneur.

Today, he resides in Coral Gables, Florida, and is an artist, photographer, avid yogi (RYT 200), CrossFitter, kite surfer, and an active dive volunteer and former board member of the Coral Restoration Foundation.

Made in the USA
Middletown, DE
12 July 2021

44018765R00177